# Chronicles of the Royal Borough of Woodstock.

COMPILED FROM THE BOROUGH RECORDS AND OTHER ORIGINAL DOCUMENTS.

BY

ADOLPHUS BALLARD, B.A., LL.B.,

Town Clerk of Woodstock.

Author of " Notes on the History of Chipping Norton."

THE CORPORATION SEAL, A.D. 1461.

Oxford:

ALDEN & COMPANY, Ltd., BOCARDO PRESS.

LONDON: SIMPKIN, MARSHALL, HAMILTON, KENT & CO. LTD.

1896

To Her Grace

CONSUELO

DUCHESS OF MARLBOROUGH

IS RESPECTFULLY DEDICATED

THIS HISTORY

OF THE LITTLE TOWN

AT THE GATES OF HER NEW HOME.

PREFACE.

THIS book is in no way a rival to the Rev. Edward Marshall's "Early History of Woodstock Manor." We have had different objects in view : his aim was to narrate the many important historical events that took place at the Royal Palace and in the neighbourhood, and to throw light on the history of the various men and women mentioned in the course of his work : and his references to the Borough of Woodstock and its inhabitants were but slight and incidental. My aim—a much humbler one—has been to write the history of the institutions of the Borough, and to show how in the past the working men and women who lived therein grappled with the every-day problems of existence. For that reason my references to the Royal Palace and Ducal Mansion are but slight and incidental, and many important events which took place have been passed over in silence. To add anything to what Mr. Marshall has written would be an impossible task.

The Borough documents in my custody have been the chief material on which this book is based ; and I have to express my grateful thanks to the Mayor and Council of the

Borough for their unanimous permission to make use of these documents, and also for permission to copy the initial letter and seal which form respectively the frontispiece and vignette to this book.

A reference to the index will show the amount of my indebtedness to the Rev. E. Marshall, from whose researches I have derived much assistance. I have also to acknowledge my obligations to the late Rev. Arthur Majendie, and to the Rev. J. E. G. Farmer, Rectors of Bladon-cum-Woodstock, for placing at my disposal the Registers and Vestry Minutes. Much help has been given me by Rev. Dr. Yule, Rector of Shipton-on-Cherwell, especially on ecclesiastical matters; and by Sir William Markby, K.C.I.E., Bursar of Balliol College, and by G. E. Baker, Esq., M.A., Bursar of Magdalen College, Oxford, who have allowed me to consult the Registers of the Archives of their respective Colleges. To Mr. Hugh Hall I am indebted for access to the files of the *Oxford Journal.* I have also to thank Mr. Councillor Prescott for permission to reproduce his excellent photograph of the Borough Mace (page 90), and Mr. J. N. Godden and Mr. W. R. Pratt for many interesting traditions. Dr. Plot's view of the Manor House, and the view of the Marketplace in 1777, are reproduced by permission of Messrs. Parker & Co., Oxford, from the plates which appeared in Marshall's "Early History of Woodstock Manor." Last, but by no means least, I shall never forget the kind assistance rendered me by my valued friend and publisher, Mr. E. C. Alden.

A. B.

WOODSTOCK, *28th March, 1896.*

CONTENTS.

LIST OF ILLUSTRATIONS.

WOODSTOCK MANOR HOUSE.

CHAPTER I.

Early History.

SINCE the Railway has been opened from the Great Western main line at Kidlington to the ancient Borough of Woodstock, not a few travellers who have found their way to the station of " Blenheim and Woodstock " have wondered at the curious blending of the names. But whoever was the godfather of the station has followed the teaching of history in giving precedence to that partner which at first sight seems the junior ; for under its older name of Woodstock Park our monarchs, for centuries before Queen Anne's time, knew and loved that country which we know as Blenheim Park ; and, as we

B

shall shortly see, the town of Woodstock was called into being by the frequent visits of the Court to Woodstock Manor House.

Our early kings were passionately fond of the chase: the Saxon Chronicle, it will be remembered, says that William the Conqueror loved the tall stags as if he were their father; and where throughout the length and breadth of England was situated a more suitable place for the indulgence of this passion than Woodstock? The forests of Woodstock, Cornbury, and Wychwood were close at hand, and stretched away for twelve miles to the west; and only a few miles away on the high land to the south of the Cherwell valley were the forests of Stowood and Shotover. So late as Domesday Book these five forests covered an area of nine leagues square, in which there were only four and a half hides (540 acres) of cultivated land, occupied by six villein tenants and eight cottagers.[a]   At the time of the Domesday Book the villages of Bladon, Combe, Stonesfield, and Wootton were very sparsely populated; while Finstock, Fawler, Ramsden, and Leafield did not exist.   The Roman villa at Northleigh, and the Roman road known as the Akeman Street passing through the Park about one mile to the north of Woodstock, are the only relics of our Latin conquerors in the neighbourhood, while the circular encampment in Bladon parish, known as the Round Hill, may perhaps be of Celtic origin.

The name—Woodstock—is Saxon, and means a woody place; and tradition points to Saxon times as those from which the Royal residence dates.   Dr. Plot[b] says that a note

[a] Domesday Book, p. 155.   [b] Plot's Oxfordshire, p. 367.

in a MS. of King Alfred the Great's translation of "Boethius De Consolatione Philosophiæ" in the Cottonian Library, states that it was completed at Woodstock; and the present Bishop of Oxford prints in his "Select Charters"* an ordinance made at Woodstock by Ethelred (the Unready) and his witan.

History records no visit of William the Conqueror to Woodstock, but the Chronicles tell us that his son Henry I built a stone wall, seven miles in circumference, round the park, and one adds that very many farms were pulled down on that account—a statement which is an obvious exaggeration, for it is recorded in Domesday Book that there were only fourteen agricultural tenants in the whole of the five forests thirty years before this time. Henry of Malmesbury goes on to tell that the King kept in the park a collection of strange beasts from foreign parts, which he had begged from foreign princes, of which the chief attraction was a porcupine. Henry of Huntingdon leads us to believe that it was Henry I who founded Old Woodstock, which is a hamlet of the parish of Wootton lying alongside the Park wall immediately to the north of the town, from which it is separated by the river Glyme. Old Woodstock was never within the Borough of New Woodstock.

It is, however, with the reign of Henry II that the history of the town of Woodstock begins. Every one has heard of the loves of that king and Fair Rosamund; some affect to doubt the story, but these latter-day sceptics appear to have forgotten that within a little over a century after her time a jury of Woodstock men returned their

* Stubbs : Select Charters, p. 72.

sworn information to Edward I that King Henry " le veyl " often sojourned at the Manor House at Woodstock " for the love of a certain woman called Rosamund."[4] True, the legends vary in different particulars, but is there any historical personage about whom varying legends have not come down to us? The historians seem to be agreed that she was one of the family of the Cliffords of Clifford Castle in Herefordshire, of whom Lord Clifford of Chudleigh is the present representative; and that she had a son, William Longespée or Longsword by name, who afterwards married the heiress of William, Earl of Salisbury. Lord Tennyson is in error when in his play of " Becket " he gives the name of Geoffrey to Rosamund's son; Geoffrey, who was made Bishop of Lincoln before he was of age, was the son of the King and a woman named Ikenai or Hikenai. The legends are agreed in saying that when Rosamund lived at Woodstock she was hidden in a maze near the Manor House, and that Queen Eleanor discovered her hiding-place by following the clue afforded by the unravelling of a skein of silk. Some say that she was unwittingly betrayed by the King, on whose spur one end of the skein had caught as he was leaving her; while others tell us that she herself when running to hide from the Queen caught her foot in the silk and dragged it after her along the mazy paths. Again there are various accounts of her death; some, and they the later historians, say that the jealous Queen got rid of her rival by poison; but the better opinion seems to be that she retired to Godstow Nunnery near Oxford, and there " in

[4] Hundred Rolls, ii, 839. See also Marshall's Early History of Woodstock Manor, pp. 49-57, for the whole history of Rosamund.

the odour of sanctity died."* At all events, it was there that
she was buried ; for when in 1191 Hugh, Bishop of Lincoln,
in whose diocese Oxford was at that time, visited Godstow,
he found a tomb in the chapel covered with a silk pall and
provided with lighted candles: on hearing whose tomb it
was, he ordered the pall and candles to be taken away, and
the body to be buried outside the chapel. After a time
the body was restored to its former tomb, which was not
destroyed till the dissolution of monasteries, when, according
to Leland, the bones were found to be enclosed in a leaden
coffin, and "when it was openid a very swete smell came
out of it." But it would be vain to visit Godstow to find
traces of Fair Rosamund, for the existing remains of the
Nunnery include no portion of its chapel, which is now
pulled down, and the road passes over its site.

The maze in which Rosamund was hidden was long ago
destroyed, but the traditional site of her hiding-place is
now marked by a Well called by her name on the left
of the northern end of the Great Bridge. It must be
remembered, however, that the landscape on which she
gazed was far different from that which meets our view
to-day. The lake did not then exist, and where now there
is a wide expanse of water were then a number of rich
water meadows through the midst of which flowed the river
Glyme.

The Manor House stood on the little eminence to the
north of the Bridge, where now stands a clump of sycamores.

* Her traditional epitaph, it will be remembered, ran thus : —
　　"Hic jacet in tumba Rosa mundi, non Rosa munda ;
　　Non redolet sed olet, quæ redolere solet."

When in 1652 Parliament ordered it to be sold it was described[f] as having three court-yards; the first, which appears to have been the most westerly, and was three-quarters of an acre in extent, was surrounded by the Gatehouse (which was probably on the south), the Prince's lodgings on the north, and a spacious church-like Hall, the

Chapel, and the Bishop's lodgings on the east; adjoining the hall was the Wardrobe court of half-an-acre in extent, which was surrounded by the Lord Chamberlain's lodgings, the wardrobe rooms, the Queen's Hall, the Steward's lodgings, the guard chamber, the presence chamber, the privy chamber looking over the tennis court into the town,[g]

[f] Parliamentary Surveys in Record Office, quoted by Marshall, p. 207.

[g] Marshall, p. 190. The illustration at the head of this chapter, which has been drawn from the best available sources, represents the Manor House as it appeared in the seventeenth century, probably from the north side.

the King's private apartments, and the Queen's lodgings. There was also a small private garden of one-eighth of an acre in extent, and the Pastry court surrounded by two large kitchens and other buildings. It is not probable that all this range of buildings existed in the reign of Henry II; in fact John Aubrey[h] tells us that the buildings on the south and west were built by Henry VII, as could be seen from the shape of the windows, and his initials displayed thereon. Like Windsor Castle, Woodstock House in its complete state was the work of many monarchs. The view of Woodstock Park given in Dr. Plot's history of Oxfordshire[i] shows us that towards the end of the seventeenth century there was a causeway leading across the meadows from the town to the south side of the Manor House, and further leads us to believe that the level of the ground on either side of the great bridge was considerably raised when Sir John Vanbrugh built it in the eighteenth century.

Fair Rosamund is an important personage in the history of Woodstock for other than romantic reasons. We have already noticed the jury of Woodstock men who returned their sworn information that King Henry had visited the Manor House "for the love of a certain woman named Rosamund." They further presented to the King that "at that time there was a certain waste place without the said park and manor; and because the men of the said King were lodged too far from the manor house aforesaid, the said Lord the King with the unanimous assent and counsel

[h] MS. Notes to Plot's Oxfordshire in the Bodleian Library, Ashm. 1722.

[i] The plate was given in Marshall's Early History of Woodstock Manor, and is reproduced in chapter v. of the present work.

of his nobles gave and granted divers parcels of land of the said waste place to divers men to build hostelries there for the use of the men of the same King."[j] They further declared that King Henry established a weekly market on Tuesday, of which his bailiff collected the toll, and that his son John established a fair for three days at the feast of St. Matthew.[k]

When the survey contained in the Hundred Rolls (from which the above extracts are taken) was made in 1279, there were 137 houses standing in the town, from which, and from sundry closes, pigstyes, shambles and gardens, the King's bailiff collected rents to the amount of 45s. 3½d. The Rolls contain the names of only 108 different householders, but it seems that some of these maintained two or more separate establishments, and it is probable that the population of the town was at least 540 in 1279. The highest rent then paid for any house was eighteenpence, which was paid by John atte Green for the house opposite the stone cross, which, till the middle of last century, stood where now stands the Town Hall;[l] for the houses on each side of the Park Gate, Edmund the Mazun and Robert the Marshal paid fourpence and fourpence halfpenny respectively; for the house on the Green between the two lanes (the Corporation garden in Back Lane) Henry Brown paid fourpence a year. In 1517 the lane leading from the High Street into the Green was called Petty John's Lane, and for a house in this lane in 1279 Margery the widow of Thomas

[j] The fact that the area of the Borough of New Woodstock was only about thirty acres can easily be explained when it is remembered that the town was built on an odd piece of waste land.

[k] Hundred Rolls, ii, 839.   [l] See plate in chap. viii.

the Parker paid a yearly rent of fourpence halfpenny. Agnes · Marmyun paid threepence for a cottage on the south side of the cemetery, and Walter the Miller his wife and mother paid twopence for the corner house in the lane opposite the butchers' shambles; for the house on the other side of the same lane, with a furnace, garden, two stalls and a smithy, Adam Beneyth paid fourpence halfpenny a year. This Adam Beneyth seems to have been a rich man, for he owned also two houses adjoining the smithy (possibly on the site of Fletcher's House), another house which was probably on the other side of Park Street, two or three tenements which cannot be located, a croft of land at Goldyngswell, and another smithy and piece of waste land, for which he paid three-halfpence, in Middle Street. For a bakery Christiana of Hensington paid one penny a year, and the like rent was paid by Agnes Siber for an oven at the east side of the cemetery well; while there were seventeen shambles where flesh was sold, which were let at one penny each, and several pigstyes, for each of which the rent was a halfpenny a year. The great contrast between then and now is illustrated by the following entry : " Agnes Batecok is tenant of a house there on condition of rendering to our Lord the King one pound of cinnamon, and of maintaining one lamp in the chapel of the said Manor House of our Lord the King every year."

The following list of names shows that at that time a large number of tradesmen lived in the town :—Henry le Yronmongare, Humphrey Pistor (the baker), Robert le Taylor, Richard le Carpenter, John le Deyere, Adam le Sclattere, Thomas le Harper, Sarra le Sumener, Gilbert

Faber (the smith), Peter le Tanner, Walter Textor (the weaver), Alfred le Turner, Richard le Viniter, Jordan le Nappere, Stephen the Parchemyner, Ralph le Cachepol, Reginald le Thechare, Thomas le Plomer, John le Wymplere, William le Pottare, and Thomas le Chapman; while there were three or four families each of Parkers and Mareschalli (marshals). Other inhabitants were distinguished by the names of their native places : Alan of Hensington, John of Clevely, John of Charlbury, Simon of Aylesbury, William of Norton, and Richard of Hampton may be cited as examples.

The survey also casually mentions the bell tower and the burial ground, and reveals to us that the Church of St. Mary Magdalene had been founded before the end of the thirteenth century. There is a good Norman doorway in the south wall, and there are Early English windows in the south aisle. But it must be borne in mind that Woodstock is ecclesiastically in the parish of Bladon, and that St. Mary's at Woodstock is merely a chapel belonging to St. Martin's at Bladon. It may be conjectured that the church was first built at the same time as the town was founded, in order that the inhabitants of Woodstock might not be obliged to walk two miles across the forest to attend the Parish Church at Bladon. Warton says that King John founded the Chantry of St. Margaret's in Woodstock Church for one priest to celebrate for his soul;[m] but the report of the Commissioners of the first year of Edward VI says that the Chantry of St. Margaret was founded by Edward Croft.[n] We are not told the date when Edward

[m] Marshall, p. 67.   [n] Ib., p. 273.

Croft founded the Chantry; but is it not possible that he lived in the reign of John? The Hundred Rolls mention Nicholas the Clerk as then living at Woodstock; so that if he was priest of St. Margaret's Chantry there was thus early a resident priest in the town.

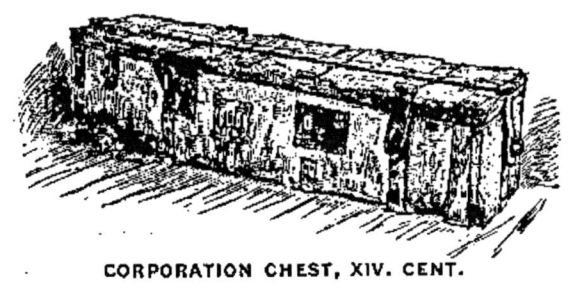

CORPORATION CHEST, XIV. CENT.

CHAPTER II.

Growth.

FROM the time of the Hundred Rolls till the middle of the fifteenth century we have little information about the growth of the town. It was considered important enough to send two Members to Parliament in 1302 and again in 1305; its representatives to the former Parliament were Edward de Parco and John Beneit,[a] and to the latter John de Wappenham and Reginald Bene; but the inhabitants of the Borough did not again exercise the Parliamentary franchise till the reign of Queen Mary. When in 1377 a poll tax of fourpence a head from every lay person male and female above the age of fourteen years was granted to Edward III, the constables of Woodstock paid to Richard Chamberlain, the collector for the County of Oxford, the sum of 54s. 4d., being the amount collected from 164 adults living at Woodstock.[b] If the number of

---

[a] Was he the son of Adam Beneyth noted at p. 9 ?

[b] Lay Subsidy Rolls, $\frac{161}{41}$.

those under fourteen is taken as one-third of the population and one-half is added to the amount, as suggested by the late Professor Thorold Rogers,[c] we are able to fix the population of Woodstock in 1377 at 255, showing a decrease of 285 within the century since the Hundred Rolls. This is not improbable, when we remember that England had been devastated by the Black Death during the reign of Edward III, and that the effects of the disease were felt most severely among the poor.[d] That Woodstock was not a rich town is shown by the fact that in 1327, when a tax of a twentieth (five per cent.) was levied by Edward III, only eighteen persons in the town were assessed, and their payments ranged from 5s. 3d. down to one shilling.

The house on the north of the Park Gate is known as Chaucer's House ; and there is a tradition that it was once the property of "the Father of English Poetry"; indeed some enthusiasts have professed to identify Woodstock Park in his description of scenery. But Mr. Marshall has shown conclusively that although that house may have belonged to his son, Thomas Chaucer, who received a grant of the manor in 1411, yet it is morally certain that it never belonged to the poet.[e]

Although the town of Woodstock was small and poor in

---

[c] Six Centuries of Work and Wages, p. 117.

[d] The whole neighbourhood seems to have suffered in the same proportion. Tackley had forty householders—a population of 200—in 1279, but only sixty-four paid the poll tax of 1377. If, as above, we add one-half to the latter number, we find that the population had decreased by 104 ; similarly the population of Thrupp had decreased from 80 (16 × 5) to 60 (40 + 20).

[e] Marshall, c. vii.

the fourteenth century, yet it was probably of no small
importance. The first charter granted by Henry VI in 1453
recited that "Our beloved Tenants of our Vill of New
Woodstock in the County of Oxford, which is of the ancient
demesne of our Crown, and the Residents and Inhabitants
of the same Vill have represented to Us after what manner
themselves and such Tenants, Residents and Inhabitants
have for no short time past [*non modico tempore transacto*]
used and enjoyed certain Liberties and Free Customs."
We have no definite information about the nature of these
Liberties and Free Customs, except that from other
sources we learn that there was a custom that the transfer
of any house or landed property within the Borough
should be proclaimed before the Mayor, Aldermen, and
Burgesses in the Portmouth or Borough Court on three
consecutive court days, and if no one appeared to challenge
the purchaser's title all claimants were thereafter barred.
Now the earliest document in the Borough safe is a
Memorandum, under the Borough seal, of such proclamations in the first year of the reign of Edward IV (1461).
And the oldest book in the possession of the Corporation
(a parchment volume with very worm-eaten board covers)
contains a series of memoranda of such proclamations
dating from 35 Hen. VI (1456) to 19 Eliz. (1577), each
of which recites that the custom existed from time whereof
the memory of man runneth not to the contrary. If the
records are to be trusted that no man could remember the
origin of this custom, it is clear that the custom is one of
those referred to in the charter as having been enjoyed by
the inhabitants of the Borough "for no short time past."

The fact that all these memoranda refer to the proclamation of the transfer before the Mayor and Aldermen leads us to believe that these officials existed in the town previously to Henry's Charter,—a belief which is supported by the occurrence of the name of "Robert Stevenys, Mayor of Wodestoke," as a witness to a lease of the year 1435, now in the possession of Magdalen College, Oxford.[']

Whatever may have been the nature of the prescriptive Corporation that had thitherto existed, the Charter alleges "that the said Tenants, Residents and Inhabitants, fearing for the time to come that they would be aggrieved, molested, and disturbed in such their Liberties and Free Customs for want of their being expressed, and in their other actions had most humbly besought Us graciously to grant to the same Tenants, Residents and Inhabitants and to their heirs and successors the Liberties and Free Customs aforesaid, together with the other privileges, franchises and exemptions following expressed in special terms, and to incorporate them in form and manner following." Thereupon the King, "being favourably inclined to the Petition of the same Tenants, Residents and Inhabitants in this behalf, and of his especial grace," proceeded to grant them a Charter in the usual terms of the day.

First of all he granted that the Vill of New Woodstock should be a Free Borough, then that the inhabitants should be free Burgesses, that they should have a Merchant Guild

['] Since this chapter was in the press I have been able, through the kindness of Sir William Markby, to consult the archives of Balliol College. Among them are three deeds of earlier date, to which the name of the Mayor of Woodstock for the time being appears as a witness. The three Mayors are :—1398, Edmund Mundi ; 1407, Thomas Orleton ; 1414, Nicholas Blakhalle.

and enjoy the same Liberties and Free Customs as the Burgesses of New Windsor.

The members of the Merchant Guild were alone allowed to trade within the Borough; the nature of their claim is best explained by the following extract from a charter of Edward III to the City of Oxford:—"And that no one who is not of their Guild shall sell any wine or mercery or any goods whatsoever within the said City of Oxford or its suburbs by retail."[g]

The privileges conferred by the grant that the town should be a Free Borough appear to have been those which are expressly conferred by the charter. In the first place they were to be a body corporate by the name of the Mayor and Commonalty of the Vill of New Woodstock, with perpetual succession and a Common Seal;[h] and the Commonalty were to choose a Mayor and a Sergeant-at-Mace to rule and govern them for ever; but the charter makes no mention of the Aldermen or of a Council. Then there were provisions which established an independent Borough Court for the trial of all civil actions and criminal offences (except felonies) within the Borough, and prohibited the County Justices, Sheriffs, and Royal officers generally from enquiring into offences within the Borough or in any way interfering with

[g] Gross: Gild Merchant, ii, 192. It is perfectly clear that in the twelfth and thirteenth centuries the institutions of the Borough were distinct from those of the Guild, and that a man might live in a town without belonging to the Merchant Guild of that town, and, *vice versa*, that a man might belong to the Merchant Guild although he did not live in the town.—Gross, i, c. v.

[h] The Common Seal has varied from time to time: the variation in the arms is but slight; but the crest, which in 1461 was a knight's helmet (see vignette on title-page) had by 1634 been changed into a ducal coronet.

the affairs of the town. A gain of no less importance was that the King granted to the Mayor and Commonalty the whole Borough and "a certain pool or marsh adjoining the town, and known as Le Pool," at the yearly rent of four marks; this grant implies that the rents of all the houses in the town which had thitherto been collected by the King's Bailiff were for the future to be collected by the Borough Officers. Other privileges were that the Mayor and Commonalty and their successors were to be free of toll throughout the Realm[1]; they were to receive all fines, forfeitures, waifs, strays, treasure trove, felons' goods, and other Royal perquisites within the Borough; and to make and have the assay and assize of bread and beer and other victuals, when it should be necessary. In his Charter the King made no mention of the market on Tuesday; but he confirmed the grant of the fair at the feast of St. Matthew, and granted an additional fair for five days at the feast of St. Mary Magdalen.

Three clauses of the Charter deserve further notice : the first giving to the inhabitants of the Borough the power of devising by will what each might have acquired for himself within the Borough ; the second prohibiting any man from seizing within the Borough any inhabitant whom he might claim to be his villein—a privilege which was highly valued in the days before serfdom came to an end ; and the third exempting for ever the Mayor and Commonalty from being compelled to choose any Burgesses of the Borough to come to any Parliament thereafter to be held. This exemption

[1] This exemption from toll was allowed at Oxford in the early years of this century. (Report of Mun. Corp. Com., i, 141.)

from Parliamentary representation was a privilege sought by many poor boroughs in the days when Members of Parliament received a salary. But the exemption of Woodstock lasted for only another century ; for Sir Ralph Chamberlain, Knight, and William Johnson, Esq., represented the Borough at the Parliament held at Oxford in the first year of the reign of Queen Mary ; and from 1570 till 1831 the freemen of the Borough returned two Members to the House of Commons.

This Charter of Henry VI was lost before the reign of Henry VII, and is now only known to us from its being recited in the charters of later monarchs. The first Mayor under the Charter of whom we have any record is John Anstyn, who was chief magistrate in 1456.

A few months before Henry VI granted this Charter conferring the right of self-government on the town he had made provision for the spiritual welfare of the inhabitants. It will be remembered that New Woodstock is situate in the parish of Bladon, and that the church of St. Mary at Woodstock is merely a chapel of the parish church at Bladon, which is two miles distant from the town. We cannot be certain that before this time divine service was frequently celebrated at St. Mary's Church ; there is abundant reason (as will be seen later on) for believing that in the early part of the seventeenth century, sermons were preached at the church only every third Sunday ; and even within this present century the inhabitants of New Woodstock had good cause to complain that their spiritual necessities were not adequately attended to. In order to remedy this grievance Henry VI granted letters patent to

Nicholas Newton,[j] parson of Bladon, and John Booker and John Bytan, wardens of the chapel, to acquire lands in mortmain to the value of £10 a year from any persons who might be willing to assign or bequeath the same, to the intent that the King's tenants at Woodstock might have "a certain fit chaplain to celebrate divine offices every day in the same chapel for the good estate of Us and our dear Consort while we shall live and for our souls when we shall have departed out of this life, and for the souls of all the faithful deceased." It is usually thought that the chantry founded in pursuance of these letters patent was that afterwards known as the "Chantry of our Lady," or the "Chantry of the Blessed Mary." According to the Valor Ecclesiasticus (a valuation of ecclesiastical property) made in 1535, the gross value of the property acquired under these letters patent amounted to £7 2s., net £5 5s.[k]

After Henry VI had been deposed and his rival Edward IV had been crowned King of England, the inhabitants of New Woodstock approached the new monarch and from him obtained in 1463 a confirmation of their previous charter. The earliest rent roll of the Borough is dated six years later, and is contained in the old book to which reference has been made; it shows that in 1469 there were at least a hundred and ten houses in the town, held at rents amounting to 39s. 6¾d. The George Inn and the Wine Market Street are casually mentioned in this rent roll; and mention is made of several crofts, barns, and gardens: the Brothers of St. John of Jerusalem then owned two or three houses in the town. The same book also

[j] Quoted at length by Marshall, p. 331. [k] Ib., p. 333.

contains the earliest account of the Borough Finances,
which is dated 1519: the gross revenue of the borough in
that year amounted to 55s. 2d., which included 20s. the
rent of the Common Pool, 4s. the rent of two shops under
the Guild Hall, and 2s. 4d. the rent of the Spyttell House
Close.[1] The expenditure amounted to 34s. 6d., and included the following item :—

> "For making of ii payers of stooks (stocks)
>   a cokyng (cucking) stoole and all things
>   necessarie for the same   ...   ...   ixs."

There was also a sum of 13s. 4d. allowed to the tenants
of the Common Pool because of the damage "to the
herbage of the said pool this year done by the horses of
certain of the King's servants by the procurement of
certain misgoverned persons of the town." It should be
noticed that the house rents, forfeitures, and waifs and strays
are not set down on the receipt side of these accounts, nor
is the fee farm rent set down on the payment side ; the
reason for these omissions is that till 1580 the rents, etc.,
were received by the Mayor, who thereout paid the fee
farm rent and took for himself any profit that there might
be. On the opposite page to that containing the account
is a list of the Mayor, Aldermen, Councillors, and Freemen
of the Borough in that year, 1519: William Wyse was
Mayor, and there were four Aldermen and thirteen
Councillors, two of whom were the Chamberlains ; but
there is no mention of the Town Clerk, nor of the Sergeant-
at-Mace, nor is there a single name on this list that is
to be found on the Burgess Roll of to-day.

[1] Now the garden of Chaucer's House.

In the mayoralty of Thomas Fletcher (1535) it was agreed by the Common Council that William Marshall, Priest, should have the yearly wage of eight marks, "and he shall dayle pray for the founder and iiii tymes a yere .... syng and say masse, and then at any of the seid iiii tymes Reherse and pray by name for all of the bene-factors and donors of the rentts and lands to the maynteiñce of his benefice."

By Acts of Parliament of the last year of the reign of Henry VIII and the first year of Edward VI, all colleges, free chapels, chantries, and guilds having perpetuity for ever within the realm were dissolved and their possessions were seized into the King's hands; hence the property belonging to the chantry of the Blessed Mary at Woodstock became vested in the Crown, and from a return of the Commissioners appointed by Edward the Sixth[m] it appears that in 1547 the value of such property amounted to £10 17s. 4d. gross, £10 13s. 4½d. net, and that the whole income had been received by Sir[n] Martin Cave, "a man very well learned and mete to kepe a cure," who had no other living. This return also refers to "The Chauntry of Saint Margaretts," which we have already noticed as having been founded by Edward Croft, Esq., and was then of the gross value of £8 9s., net £7 13s. 10½d.; all the income had been received by Sir[n] Edward Jones, who had no other living. Incidentally the return informs us that the "houseling people" in the town numbered 760 in 1547.

---

[m] Marshall, p. 372.

[n] All clergymen then had the title "Sir." Every one remembers Sir Oliver Martext in "As You Like It."

As King Edward VI, or rather his advisers, were in great want of ready money, much of the property which came to the Crown from the dissolution of the chantries and guilds was sold in a very short time. Thus in 1549 a man named Venables purchased part of the possessions of the Chantry of the Blessed Mary, consisting of four houses—one in Oxford Street, two in High Street, and one in the Middle Ward—let at 30s. a year[o]; then in 1553 John Wright and Thomas Holmes purchased other part of the possessions of the Chantry of the Blessed Mary, consisting of five houses —one known as the Chantry House, one in Oxford Street, one in High Street, and two, the situation of which is unspecified, let at £2 5s. 4d.: but it is suggested that Wright and Holmes purchased these properties as trustees for the Duke of Suffolk, who was beheaded by Queen Mary[p]; and in 1565 other part of the possessions of this Chantry was given to the town by Queen Elizabeth. The property of the Chantry of St. Margaret was sold in 1548 to George Owen and William Martin; it consisted of eight houses in Woodstock, the brewhouse in Old Woodstock, a house in Wootton, another at Weston, and certain lands at Hensington and Shipton, the whole of the annual value of £7 15s. 8d.[q] Hence it appears that for some years prior to the Reformation two priests were resident in the town; but that after the disestablishment and disendowment of the Chantries, the inhabitants of the Borough were again left to the occasional ministrations of the Rector of Bladon.

The old book to which reference has already been made contains sundry orders for the good government of the

[o] Marshall, p. 359.   [p] Ib., p. 360.   [q] Ib., p. 367.

town; thus in 1548 all the inhabitants are stated to have gathered in Convocation and to have agreed that "every year at Michaelmas even they shall be gathered together at the Guild Hall . . . . . that then whomsoever the Commons assembled or the most part of them shall . . . . . . choose to be their said Mayor shall take it upon him . . . . . . "; thus showing that at that time the Mayor was elected at an open meeting of the inhabitants. Following the above order are four "Ordinances made by the XII," probably by the Council; while after these is found a law made at a "Common Assembly" in the Guild Hall, in the year 1557, that no one should be admitted to dwell within the town or to be a freeman unless he was able to bear scot and lot [pay his rates] and all other charges, or a freeman was bound for him. In 1568 the Mayor, Aldermen and Common Council forbad any freeman of the borough to sue another freeman elsewhere than in the Borough Court, under a penalty of £10; and in the next year an escheat that had fallen to the town was granted to George Whitton.

It should be remembered that from May, 1554, until April, 1555, the Princess Elizabeth was imprisoned at the Gate House of Woodstock Manor. She had been accused of being an accomplice in the rebellion headed by Wyat against her half sister, Queen Mary, and on that account had been committed to the Tower, but nothing could be proved against her. It is alleged that she was treated with harshness by her gaolers at Woodstock; certainly she was not allowed to go out of the gardens and courts enclosed in the Manor House, her letters were read by her keepers, and no stranger was allowed to converse with her out of the hearing of Sir Henry Bedingfield, to whom she was given in charge; but compared with the treatment suffered by most political prisoners of the time her lot was exceptionally easy and favoured. The Queen's physicians were sent to attend her during an illness; and she was allowed to spend Christmas at Hampton Court.

There is a tradition at Woodstock that the inhabitants of the Borough treated her with great courtesy during her imprisonment; and that on her accession to the Crown she promised to make them a present " in token of the happy change in my circumstances." Certain it is that in the first year of her reign she confirmed the Charter of Henry VI, which had been previously confirmed by both Henry VII and Edward VI; and in 1565 she gave to the town four shops, thirteen cottages, and certain rents, amounting to 15s. 8d., which had formerly belonged to the Chantry of the Blessed Mary in Woodstock; but although the yearly value of this property was £3 17s. 7½d., out of which had to be paid two rent-charges, the one to Jeremy Westall, of 2s. 4d., and the other of 5s. 4½d. to Francis Chamberlain, the Queen reserved to herself an annual rent of £4, and thus secured the best of the bargain.[r] Some of the houses given to the town at this time can be identified; among them were the properties now known as the King's Arms and the Woodstock Arms, Magdalen House in the Holloway (which stood on the south side of the street, and was pulled down about sixty years ago to widen the road), and the Corporation property in Brown's Lane. There were also

---

[r] The initial letter of Queen Elizabeth's Charter is reproduced as a frontispiece to this volume.

some houses standing between St. Mary's Church and the street ; some of which were sold by the Corporation to Mr. Edmund Hiorne in 1618.

The Queen further granted to the Mayor and Commonalty the right to hold a market on Friday, and two fairs of four days each at the Feast of St. Nicholas and at Lady Day, for which she was to receive the additional rent of £1 6s. 8d. a year. According to this Charter the Mayor was to hold a court of "pie powder" for the trial of offences at the fairs, and also to have the profits arising from the weighing of the wool and yarn brought to the market ; and it was ordered that the same weights should be used in weighing wool and yarn at Woodstock as were used at Cirencester. During the first half of the seventeenth century the wool beam was let by the Mayor and Commonalty to various individuals at rents varying from twenty to four-and-twenty shillings a year. In 1576 an Act of Parliament was passed whereby it was enacted that it should "be lawful for every person to buy and sell within the Borough of Woodstock all manner of wools and yarns brought into the Borough on the usual market and fair days."* Five years later a Bill was introduced into the House for the re-edifying of the Borough of New Woodstock, but although it passed its first and second reading it was, to use the language of the Journals of the House, "dashed" at its third reading.*

* 18 Eliz., c. 21.   * Journals H. C., i. 128.

CHAPTER III.

The Constitution of 1580.

NEXT to the old book previously referred to, and some charters and old conveyances, the oldest record belonging to the borough is a parchment book, bound in oak boards and secured by ancient locks. This book contains the "Orders made, concluded, enacted, establishedd, and agreed uppon by the condiscent assent and agreement of the Maior, Aldermen, and Comon Counsell of the said Burrough for the quyet and civill government of themselves and the Comynaltie of the same Burrough" on the 10th March and 17th September, 1580, "in the time of William Skellton, Maior there." From this document we learn that great changes had taken place in the previous century and a quarter. For, instead of the two officials named in the Charter of Henry VI—the Mayor and Sergeant-at-Mace—in the interval there had grown up a large and complicated Corporation, consisting of a High Steward, Recorder, Mayor, six Aldermen (one of whom was to be Mayor), twenty Common Councillors, Town Clerk, Cryer of the Court, and Sergeant-at-Mace, most of whom were elected for life. Unfortunately we have no information concerning the various stages in the growth of this new body, which with slight modifications received the sanction of the Crown by a Charter of Charles II in 1665, and existed thenceforth until 1886.

These Orders are worthy of study, inasmuch as they reveal to us that the Charter of Charles II (which for two centuries was regarded as the governing Charter of the Borough) merely gave the Royal Assent to a body of customs which had grown up in the previous centuries, and did not create a new constitution. Only one or two additional powers were conferred on the Corporation by Charles's Charter, and on the other hand there are several powers given by the Charter of Henry VI, of which it makes no mention. To thoroughly understand the orders of 1580 is to understand the constitution of the Borough for the next three centuries, and therefore it is expedient to consider them systematically.

A.—THE FREEMEN.

In 1580 the Merchant Guild had ceased to exist in name, but the monopoly of trading possessed by its members was maintained by the orders which forbade others than freemen from trading within the Borough. The following is the order bearing on the point :—

"Item, it is enacted, ordered, and decreed that no
person not beinge a freeman of this borrough shall
use or exercise anye occupacon or trade openlie

or privilie within this burrough unles he worke for
a freeman and beinge lawfullye hyred uppon paine to
. forfett and pay to thuse of the towne for everye
defaulte to the contrarye vis. viii*d*. to be levied
lykewise by distres."

Furthermore, no freeman was to maintain any man not
being free of the Borough in any trade or occupation under
colour of him, un.ess he had previously hired him for one
whole year before the Mayor ; nor was a freeman to allow
any "forryner" to work in his house unless he had lawfully
hired him, under penalties of twenty shillings for each
offence. And until the middle of this century, so long as
any freeman continued to be admitted, some memory of
these orders was preserved in the freeman's oath, which
was administered at his admission, and contained the
following paragraph :—

"And you shall not by colour of your Freedom bear out
or cover under you any foreign Person or Stranger,
but according to the best of your skill, wit, cunning
and power you shall uphold and maintain all the
Liberties, Franchises, good Customs, Orders, and
Usages of this Town and Corporation."

The memorandum in the Borough Records of the admission of freemen in the sixteenth century is that they were
admitted to the liberties and franchises of the Borough ;
in 1580 there are two memoranda that certain persons
were admitted to the liberties, franchises, and *guild* of the
Borough ; then the old formula occurs again for a few years,
until in 1601 the record is that a certain man is sworn a
"liber homo" or freeman of the Borough.

It has been already stated that it was not necessary that every member of the Merchant Guild should reside in the town ; this was also true of the freemen of Woodstock. The orders of 1580 recognise that freemen might reside out of the town, and provide that "everye forren freeman of the burrough not dwelling within the same shall have allwayes within this borrough a pawne worth ffortye shillings whereof the Mayor and the Chamberlens to be made pryvie uppon payne to be disfranchysed within one month nexte after warninge. And the same pawne to be straynable." In 1662 there were ten foreign freemen, and to-day, out of a total of seven freemen, six reside without the town.

It was no easy task to preserve the trading privileges of the freemen ; and on 2nd May, 1704, the Council resolved to "assist the freemen of this Corporation that are inhabitants (so far as by law they may) to keep out all persons that are not free, from following any trade or working at any trade or manual occupation in this Town, the Tradesmen bearing the charge of any suit that may arise thereupon ; and that bye-laws be made accordingly." On the 16th of December, 1723, the Corporation agreed "that advice be taken whether making ourselves a Company will keep out all traders that are not free of such Company, and if it is the opinion of Counsel that it will be effectual that proper methods be taken to procure such Charter at the Corporation charge." But the only record of proceedings under these orders is of those at the View of Frankpledge and Petty Sessions on 4th October, 1728, when John Kempter, having been "indicted for following the Trade of a Taylor in the Borough not being free, appeared, pleaded guilty, and paid for a fine one shilling, and Francis Murrin for the same offence paid 3s. 4d." : and the monopoly had quite broken down by the beginning of this century. This inability to preserve the rights of the freemen at Woodstock is the more remarkable when we bear in mind that until the Municipal Corporations Act of 1835 the freemen of the neighbouring borough of Chipping Norton maintained their trading monopoly to the full."

This monopoly of trading, possessed by the Freemen in 1580, is not the only evidence that they represented the members of the old Merchant Guild; for we find that admission to their ranks was obtained in ways similar to those by which men became members of the Guild :—by birth, by seven years' apprenticeship to a freeman, by marrying a freeman's widow, or by purchase. Although by the orders of 1580 the terms of admission were fixed at a fee of £5 on the purchase of the freedom of the Borough by a foreigner, yet in practice it seems that the Corporation bargained for the best sum they could get from him, and would not disdain the small fee offered by a poor man. In 1675 George Lowe agreed to pave or pitch a portion of the Market Place, in consideration of being admitted a freeman and receiving £3 10s. from the town. In the eighteenth century it was the custom to admit gentlemen as honorary freemen upon payment of two guineas, and their ordinary fees.

In addition to the fees payable by a freeman to the Mayor, the Town Clerk, and the town, every newly elected freeman was obliged "within six weeks nexte after his

* Notes on the History of Chipping Norton, p. 18.

admittance to bringe into the gilde hall of this burrough a good and sufficient newe lether buckett there to remayne to thuse of this burrough uppon payne to forfett to thuse of the Town vi*s*. viii*d*. to be levied by distres." In later years the freemen paid 3*s*. 4*d*. each to the Chamberlains for the purchase of these buckets, and the Chamberlains accounted for these moneys at the end of their years of office. On St. Thomas's Day, 1623, there were twelve buckets in the hall, and the chamberlains had 36*s*. 8*d*. in hand to procure more; twelve years later there were seventy-two, which were given into the charge of the Cryer of the Court, and as the Chamberlains then had in hand 43*s*. 4*d*. on the "bucket account" they were ordered to procure new ladders, scaling poles, and scaling irons for the use of the town.

In addition to the monopoly of trading with the Borough there were other privileges which belonged to the freemen: they alone, as we shall see, had any voice in the government of the Borough, and were eligible to be members of the Common Council; and they alone elected the Mayor and also the two members who represented the town in Parliament. In relation to the latter privilege it should be noticed that in 1660 it was resolved by the Mayor and the major part of the Common Council that only Free Comburgesses residing within the Borough were entitled to vote at the Parliamentary election; and that no foreign freeman ought to be allowed to give his voice or consent at any time thereafter unless he first paid £1 13*s*. 4*d*. to be employed to the use of the Borough.

It should also be noticed that till the supersession of the

Corporation in 1886 the leases of the Borough property stated that they were granted by the Mayor and Commonalty[b] " by and with the assent and consent of the whole Corporation *or* Guild." In this connection the word "Corporation " includes the whole body of freemen who alone had any voice in the election of the Mayor and Council; and thus the freemen are pointed out as the representatives of the Guild. The Charter of Charles II provides that " the Council shall assemble ' in domo mercatorum,' otherwise called the Guild hall."

This concentration of all power in the hands of the freemen, who alone were allowed to trade within the Borough, and who became free of the Borough in the same manner as men had previously become members of the Merchant Guild, may perhaps indicate that the Merchant Guild had during the fifteenth and sixteenth centuries become so strong as to secure for itself the government of the town, and to deprive the other inhabitants of any share in its privileges. But there is another possible explanation. It will be remembered that by the Charter of 1453 the tenants, residents and inhabitants of the Vill of New Woodstock were declared to be free burgesses. In the present day comprehensive words like these would be held to confer the franchise on all the inhabitants, whether natives or immigrants; but it is by no means certain that the mediæval lawyers would have put this interpretation on the words,

---

[b] The Borough was incorporated by the name of " The Mayor and Commonalty of the Vill of New Woodstock"; but after the growth of the Council, as all business was transacted at Council and not at Townsmeetings, the Council seems to have appropriated the Corporate title ; but there are several instances where the word "commonalty" was used as referring to the whole body of freemen. (See Index.)

and it is possible that the inhabitants at the time of the
Charter considered that they alone were entitled to the
franchise and refused it to all immigrants. If every burgess
was a member of the Merchant Guild and *vice versâ* every
member of the Merchant Guild was a burgess,[c] it was natural
that admission to the franchise should be granted in the
same way as admission to the Merchant Guild. In that
case the "freemen" of 1580 would be the descendants of
the "inhabitants" of 1453, with the addition of those
immigrants who had purchased their freedom.

B.—THE OFFICIALS.

As has been already pointed out, the governing body of
the Borough in 1580 was very different from that established
by the Charter of Henry VI. Instead of the two officials
who alone were authorized by the charter—the Mayor and
the Sergeant-at-Mace—there was in Queen Elizabeth's time
a perfect hierarchy of officials, each of whom had his allotted
task to perform.

(1) *The Mayor* was chosen from among the Aldermen
by the freemen of the borough on the Monday before St.
Matthew's Day, and entered upon his office on the Monday
next after Michaelmas. The mode of election was as follows:
The Mayor, Aldermen and Common Council assembled at
the Guild Hall, and the Mayor chose two of the Councillors
to ascertain from every member of the whole body to which
of the Aldermen he would give his vote as Mayor for the
ensuing year, and after the votes of the Corporation had
been counted the Mayor called in the Commons (in another

[c] A not improbable conjecture, as the town was so small.

D

of the orders they are called the freemen) and showed which
two of the Aldermen had the highest number of votes: then
he was to say to them : "Those that will gyve their voyses
to thone Alderman stande of that syde and those that will
gyve their voyses to thother Alderman so nominated stande
on the other syde. And thereuppon that Alderman of the
twoe nominated which shall have most voyses of the benche
and Common Councell and Comoners shall rule as Mayor
for the yere following." This practice was followed till
1664 : for a memorandum in the Book of Acts of the
Portmouth Court tells that on the 11th May, 1629,
in consequence of the death during his mayoralty of
Mr. Alderman Meatcalfe, the then Mayor, the free comburgesses assembled at the Guild Hall to elect a new
Mayor, and there Mr. Alderman Glover was elected Mayor
" by and with the free consent of the rest of the Aldermen
Common Council and whole Commonalty of the Borough."
A similar practice had been observed in 1607 and 1610,
when the then Mayors had died during their respective
mayoralties.

Previously to 1580 the Mayor seems to have received all
the waifs and strays and other royal perquisites, and the
rent of the wool beam and other rents for his own use, and
to have discharged therefrom the fee farm rent; but by the
orders of 1580 it was decreed that he was in future to
receive a stipend of £10 to be paid half-yearly, and that the
Chamberlains were to receive the waifs and strays, etc., and
the rents, and to discharge the fee farm rent. In addition
he was entitled to fees on the admission of freemen and
to certain fees of court.

Any Mayor who had been duly elected and refused to serve was to be fined four marks, = £2 .13s. 4d.

Then, as now, the Mayor was the chief magistrate within the Borough; he was also Clerk of the Market, and as such held the Assize of Bread and Beer; and he commonly presided at the sitting of the Portmouth Court.

(2) *The High Steward* was always a gentleman of position in the neighbourhood; in 1580 Sir Henry Lee of Dytchley filled that position. His duties were not onerous, and seem to have been merely to attend at the election of the Mayor " to make an oration to the Comynaltie concerning the eleccon," and to administer the proper oaths to the Mayor; but this duty might have been performed by his deputy. He received no salary, but during the early part of the seventeenth century was usually the recipient of a Christmas gift from the Corporation, which in 1610 took the form of a cake costing 9s. and a sugar-loaf costing 9s. 10d.

(3) *The Recorder* is not named in the orders of 1580, but from the Chamberlains' accounts it appears that in 1609 a fee of £3 6s. 8d. was paid to the Recorder. He was the legal adviser of the Corporation; his opinion was often taken by them, and he always took his seat beside the Mayor at the Petty Sessions and View of Frankpledge. Both the Recorder and the High Steward were appointed by resolutions of the whole Council, and before their appointment had been made free of the Borough.

(4) *The Aldermen* were originally six in number; but a further order in 1583 reduced their number to five; nor was this latter number altered by the Charter of King

Charles. It appears that any vacancy in the Aldermanic bench was filled from the Common Council by the votes of the surviving Aldermen and the Common Councillors; though the only specific instruction was that no person was to be elected Alderman till he had served the office of Chamberlain. Under Charles' Charter the Aldermen were *ex-officio* Magistrates, and it appears that previous to that time they had acted as Justices, since the names of the five Aldermen appear in the few Commissions of the Peace for the Borough which have been preserved. They received no salary.

(5) *The Chamberlains* were two in number, and received and paid all moneys on behalf of the town. Again there are no specific instructions about their election, but it appears that they were chosen by the Aldermen and Councillors out of the Common Council. They accounted on St. Thomas's Day, and were to find sufficient surety to make a just and true account. The Chamberlains' accounts from 1609 to 1650, and from 1738 to the present day, are still in the Borough safe.

(6) *The Common Council.* From the orders of 1580 we learn that theretofore the Mayor had been used "to elect, nominate and choose at his pleasure the comon Counsell of the Burrough, and at his pleasure to disallowe them or anye of them without any consent of the Comynaltie."[d] But it was then decreed that thereafter "if the Mayor and his bretheren and the Comynaltie happen to mislyke with any-one . . . . . elected . . . . one of the Comon Counsell of this

d This was also the rule at Coventry. See Town Life in the Fifteenth Century, ii, 353.

burrough, That then such person and persons being so mislyked uppon just cause proved shalbe putt forth of the said Counsell by the comon consent of the Mayor and his bretherne and the rest of the same Counsell for that tyme being." On the 25th September, 1581, George Whitton "for his disobedience towards Mr. Mayor" was disfranchised "for that he beinge commanded upon his othe to come to Mr. Mayor uppon business for this borrough refused so to do." On the 2nd September, 1583, William Radman "for divers apparent causes" was thought by the Council not fit to be an Alderman or a freeman, and was therefore dismissed and disfranchised; and there are other records in the Acts of the Council to a similar effect.

The next order specifies that in future the number of the Common Council should be twenty, and that any vacancy should be filled by a vote of the freemen upon the names submitted to them by the Mayor, Aldermen, and surviving members of the Council.

The aldermen and common councillors had their appropriate gowns and coats, without which they were forbidden to come before the Mayor at the Guild Hall upon any business; moreover they were all obliged to attend the Mayor to church when there was any "sarmon or preachinge" and "upon all high festivall days," when the Mace was to precede them; and they were forbidden to "revyle, miscall or gyve any unfitting, undecent or obprobrious wordes to any other of the same companye" upon penalty of ten shillings to be forfeited to the use of the town. If any of the Commonalty of the Borough reviled or used opprobrious words against any of the aldermen or council-

lors, he was to be imprisoned at the discretion of the
Mayor, and to be fined 13*s*. 4*d*. The accounts for 1635
show that a sum of 3*s*. 4*d*. was " Received of John Durbridge
for a fine imposed upon him for speaking ill words of
Wm. Edwards, one of the Common Council." Any
member of the Council absenting himself from business
was to be fined 3*s*. 4*d*., and the same fine was inflicted
on every freeman who was absent from any election.

(7) *The Town Clerk* is mentioned only casually in the
orders of 1580, as being entitled to certain small fees on
the admission of freemen and for the use of the Borough
Seal. There are no directions as to the mode of his
appointment, but an examination of the records seems to
indicate that he was a member of the Common Council,
and therefore a freeman of the Borough. He was the
adviser of the Mayor in the Portmouth Court, and received
therefrom certain fees. Edmond Hiorne, who was appointed
Town Clerk in 1607 and died in 1663, was also a Justice
of the Peace for the Borough. His salary was forty
shillings a year, and he received an additional fee of five
shillings for keeping the Chamberlains' accounts.

(8) *The Sergeant-at-Mace* was the officer of the Portmouth Court, and was employed to serve the various
processes, to arrest debtors, and to levy executions. By
the order of 1580 he was obliged to find sufficient surety
for the due execution of his office, and he was allowed to
receive the tolls of the two summer fairs as his remunera-
tion ; but in 1638 he surrendered these tolls to the town,
and thereafter received the sum of £1 10*s*. as his salary.
From the records of the Portmouth Court and the Acts of

the Council it appears that the term of appointment of the Sergeant was nominally annual, but in practice the same man was appointed year after year.

(9) *The Cryer of the Court* is an official about whom not much is known ; no duties are laid down by the orders of 1580 as pertaining to him, and but for a casual notice in the Acts of the Council a year or two later we should not know of his existence. He is not mentioned in the Charter of Charles II.

C.—MISCELLANEOUS.

The orders of 1580 did not all relate to the rights of the freemen and the duties, etc., of the members of the Corporation ; several of them were concerned with the daily life of the inhabitants at large. In the first place there were a number of market regulations, but most of these appear to have been designed to keep all the trade of the town in the hands of the townspeople, and to ensure the proper payment of toll : this latter precaution was necessary because so many towns had charters which exempted them from the payment of toll throughout the realm. Thus two orders forbid the erection of sheep-pens or other stalls or the loan of stall gear to any foreigner unless he should first agree to pay toll as others did. If any inhabitant concealed any goods or victuals which any foreigner had brought within the town with intent to sell the same, he was to forfeit 6s. 8d. It was forbidden to buy fells in any place within the Borough except between Richard Lowe's corner, the Wool Market hill stone and the Corn Market hill ; and the fishmongers' stalls were ordered to be set in Oxford

Street, beginning at Walter Eborne's shop door and so on in order towards the great elm. The stalls, which were erected in the streets, were not to exceed twenty feet in' length. Finally, all the inhabitants of the town but the common bakers—Michael Mondaye, Michael Glover, and John Williams—were forbidden to bake any kind of bread to sell either on market days or fair days (cakes only excepted). The old names of the streets show what commodities were sold in the Market: in 1469 there was a Wine Market Street; later we find the Wool Market, the Corn Market, the Beast Market, the Sheep Market, the Hog Market, the Horse Fair, and Coppery Ware Street.

Other orders related to the Portmouth* Court, which was the Borough Court, and was held fortnightly before the Mayor and one of the Aldermen; here were tried all civil actions, both real and personal, and all quarrels and police cases within the Borough, except felonies. We have very little information as to the practice of the Court, but it seems that when a plaint was issued the defendant (if a

---

* The word "Portmouth" appears in the earliest records as Portmoth, thus indicating that the last syllable is connected with the word "moot." At Bury St. Edmunds and Leicester the Borough Court was called the Portmanmote. From Gross (The Gild Merchant, i, 64; see also ii, 142) we gather that the word "moot" was used with reference to the meeting of the judiciary authorities in distinction from the meeting of the Merchant Guild. (Cf. Wyclif's version of Matt. xxvii, 27: "They took Jesu in the moot hall.") In Woodstock, then, the Portmoth represents the Court of the Justices, and is (see chapter ii) of much greater antiquity than the Guild. The first mention of the Portmouth Court is in a deed of 1310 among the muniments of Magdalen College, conveying a property subject to an annual rent to the King of sixpence, to be paid "at the next general portmoot after Michaelmas"; from which it might be argued that the Court was at that time a species of rent audit. In this connection it should be noted that the chief manorial court in the Manor of Woodstock is called the Park Gate Court, and is now held in the Lodge at the Park Gate.

freeman) was arrested and brought before the Mayor, and was afterwards released on finding bail for his appearance. · No action under five shillings was to lie against a freeman, but if the plaint was for less than that amount the Mayor or Aldermen had summary jurisdiction to award a reasonable sum to the plaintiff, to be paid within a reasonable time, and in default the defendant was to lie in Court without bail till the amount was paid ; in other cases payment was enforced by seizure and sale of the debtor's goods. On the books of this Court were enrolled all indentures of apprenticeship to freemen, and occasional acknowledgments of debt ; and in this Court alone could fines be levied or recoveries suffered of tenements within the Borough.

There is only one order dealing with proceedings on the criminal side of the Court : it prescribes that the surety for any man convicted for making an assault shall pay the fine at the next Court or be imprisoned.

Two attorneys only appear to have practised in this Court ; at all events between the years 1622 and 1635 Symon James (who was also Master of the Grammar School) usually appeared for the plaintiff, and Thomas Heathen (who was Sergeant-at-Mace) for the defendant. On 28th May, 1632, Mr. Francis Gregory was admitted by the Mayor to be an attorney in the Portmouth Court during the good pleasure of the Mayor of the Borough, in the place of Mr. Symon James, deceased.

One duty then devolved on the Mayor from which he is now free : it was enacted that every person and persons whatsoever "dwelling within this borough shall keep their

places in the church as they shall be appointed by Mr.
Mayor of the Borough, upon pain that every person doing
to the contrary shall forfeit and lose for every day so offend-
ing twelve pence to the use of the town to be levied by
distress."[r]

Another order decreed that if any future Mayor permitted
the butts to be removed from the place where they then
were, he should be fined £5.   This probably refers to the
Archery butts, but all memory of them is now lost.

[r] This order is a confirmation of one made in 1575.

CHAPTER IV.

Troublous Times.

FOR a few years after the adoption of the constitution sketched in our last chapter, there were serious troubles among the inhabitants of Woodstock. There were two factions in the town : the party that upheld the new order was led by William Skelton, who was a butcher and licensed victualler,[a] and was Mayor of the Borough for October, 1579, to October, 1581, and again from October, 1582, to October, 1584 ; the leader of the other party was George Whitton, who was Surveyor of the Park, and had been M.P. for the Borough in 1571, in which year he appears to have been Mayor.[b] He asserts that his father and grandfather had both been born at Woodstock, and his father, Owen Whitton, was Mayor in 1551

---

[a] Certain Acts of Parliament forbade the election of a victualler as Mayor ; but they were constantly broken. See Mrs. Green : Town Life in the Fifteenth Century, vol. ii, p. 62.

[b] The date of Whitton's mayoralty is uncertain; it appears to be 1571, but the parchment is much worn.

and 1554. In 1580, George Whitton was an Alderman, and his name appears among those who assented to the first part of the new constitution, which was adopted in the month of March in that year ; and it was alleged that he had given his consent to the orders made in September, which contained the provisions relating to the election of the Mayor.[e]

The documents which reveal the struggle between these two factions are deposited in the British Museum and the Record Office,[d] and do not contain sufficient details or dates to enable us to compile a connected narrative of the events to which they refer : the following account, however, may be taken as fairly accurate.

Some students may find in these documents the traces of a struggle for the franchise between the Merchant Guild (or freemen) and the other inhabitants of the town ; but

[e] S.C.B.

[d] These documents are : (i) " The Answer of William Skelton, Mayor of New Woodstock, to the supplication of George Whitton ": State Papers, Elizabeth, vol. 165, No. 53 (herein referred to as S.A.) (ii) "Causes of consideration and respect of damages to be foreseen in the alteration of the Charter of Woodstock humbly tendered in the behalf of divers inhabitants of the said Town to the Right Honourable Lord Burleigh, Lord High Treasurer of England," dated 26th May, 1584 : British Museum, Lansdown MSS., vol. 40, No. 32 (herein referred to as C.C. (iii) " The Bill of Complaint and Answer thereto in the action of the Mayor and Commonalty of New Woodstock v. George Whitton and others ": Star Chamber Proceedings, 1583. 25 Eliz., vol. 77, No. 7 (herein referred to as S.C.B. and S.C.A.) No. (i) is undated, but is calendared among the documents of 1580. This is a mistake, as it contains a reference to Whitton's disfranchisement, which from the Borough Records we know to have happened in 1581 ; and a further reference to the Exchequer action, which was commenced in 1583. A more approximate date is 1584. The documents relating to the Star Chamber proceedings are very long. Whitton complains that a copy of the Mayor's Bill of Complaint fills thirty-eight sheets of paper ; but his Answer is twice as long.

a cynic would be inclined to the hypothesis that Whitton was one of the local gentry who wanted to rule the town with a high hand, and objected to be ruled by the publicans and tradesfolk ; and that as the Courts would not have listened to tales of disappointed personal ambition, he posed as the leader of the popular party and the chief opponent of the new constitution.

His first step in opposition to the Council was to claim as parcel of his manor of Hensington a certain close called Sterting Grove, and the Horse Fair and Common Acre, which were considered to be parcel and the "ancient inheritance" of the Borough. To assert this claim he and some twenty companions riotously assembled at Hensington on July 16th, 1581, and marched thence "with armour and warlike weapons, some of them having long pyked staves, swords, bucklers, daggs, and other monstrous weapons," and "riotously and unlawfully entered the said ground called Sterting Grove, and continued there for a long space," and refused to depart at the order of the Mayor but abused him and threatened to beat him, "for fear whereof the said Mayor was driven by their outrageous speeches and furious menacing to depart and suffer them to do as they listed."* It was further alleged against him that on the last day of the same month he procured about twenty persons to cut down the posts and rails enclosing Sterting Grove, on which occasion they remained there "the greater part of the same night, making great shouts and outcries to the great terror and admiration of the whole country inhabiting thereabouts."† But Whitton produced evidence to show that Skelton had

---

* These are the very words of the Bill in the Star Chamber. † Ib.

enclosed Sterting Grove by force ; although he admits that a few years previously he had thought that this close belonged to the town.[g]

Later in that same year " the said George Whitton, intending to continue and establish himself in authority among the inhabitants of the said town," got " to himself by confederacy divers of the poorer, meaner and simpler sort of people[h] to give their voices to him to be Mayor"; and when, on the 17th September, 1581, the Council proceeded to elect the Mayor under the new provisions, " he laid a plot by his confederacy himself to be chosen Mayor, but was disappointed of his premeditated and ambitious purpose for that by lawful election and by the assent of the greater part of the commonalty the election fell upon William Ryley, the said George Whitton having very few that gave their voices to him at that time[i] ; whereupon the said George Whitton uttered his grief, alleging in many choleric speeches that the election was not according to the ancient custom." He then began " to shuffle the Mayor out of his place,[j] and used him and other with unmannerly terms, and would not suffer him to speak to the people ; and the more often he was bidden to hold his peace the more he used speeches to the people saying this election is against the (freemen's) oath and old custom."

The Mayor goes on to complain to the Court of Star

[g] S.C.A.   [h] Were they inhabitants who were not freemen ?

[i] In his answer Whitton says that John Phillips was the other candidate, and that he thought that most voices had been given to him.

[j] This Whitton denies, for he says the Mayor was not in his place, but was standing '' in the middle part of the Quyer." This appears to indicate that the election took place in the church. .

Chamber that when Whitton found he did not prevail, he lost control of himself, "and broke out in these choleric speeches, beating his fists together with frowning countenance. . . . and continued his most outrageous unseemly behaviour to the great admiration and terror of the better sort of your Majesty's liege subjects," so that there was "likely to have thereof happened an outrageous, riotous, and unseemly act unless the said William Skelton and others of the Council" had persuaded the people, and it was but "narrowly avoided by gentle persuasion used to the people, they being set on fire by the malicious and evil counsel of the said George Whitton." After the election was over Whitton "departed, despitefully using unmannerly speeches to the Mayor, not meet with reverence to be uttered to your Majesty." Eight days later the Council assembled and confirmed the orders of September, 1580, and every member signed his name in witness of his assent; but Whitton's name is conspicuous by its absence, for when he was summoned by John Brace, the Sergeant-at-Mace, to attend the Council Meeting he refused to come, and was thereupon displaced from his Aldermanship. In his answer filed in the Court of Star Chamber he excused his non-attendance by saying that he knew they intended to disfranchise him, and would not attend on that account. The minutes of this meeting are signed by William Skelton, who was Mayor at the time; the new Mayor was not sworn till the Monday after Michaelmas Day.

Whitton was further accused of raising a rebellion in the High Street on the previous Palm Sunday (the year is not stated) in company with Robert Lowe and other malefactors to the number of sixteen "by estimation," who, "rejecting the fear of God and contemning your Majesty's laws," were armed with "warlike weapons," and would not disperse when ordered so to do, but abused the officers. When the Mayor and Aldermen came on the scene and demanded the cause of their assembling in this manner, Whitton did not answer, "but most despitefully made polts (*sic*) with his mouth at the Mayor, flouting the Mayor . . . . . . spitting in the Mayor's face, lifting up his leg unto him, saying, Put this leg in the stocks if thou darest, for it will become a pair of stocks full well "; and the Mayor adds "that unless great discretion had been used by the said Mayor and those with him the whole inhabitants of your said town had been in an uproar, and manslaughter or other great mischief, hurt and disturbance had ensued," but it was avoided by the Mayor charging "the people in your Majesty's name to keep your Majesty's peace."[k] Whitton's tale is that he was walking along the street and heard the Mayor on the other side of the way abusing a man, and on his going across to enquire the reason, the Mayor began to abuse him and to threaten to lay him by the heels and put him in the stocks. Whitton replied that he durst not do so as he had done nothing wrong, and took refuge in Bradshaw's house until some of the Mayor's friends had taken him home to bed; he altogether denied that there was a riot on Palm Sunday. Richard Lowe confirmed his story, and told the court that when he was going to bed that night he heard a noise under his window and "thought it was Mr. Mayor." His wife agreed with him; so he went out into the street to see what

[k] S.C.B.

was the matter, and found the Mayor "chiding the said George Whitton and giving him unseemly words." He saw the Mayor shake his fists and spit at him and threaten to "make him dance Lowe's dance"; by that Lowe understood that the Mayor wanted to put Whitton in the stocks in the same way as he had punished Lowe some three or four times previously. He asserted too that Whitton took refuge at Bradshaw's house until the Mayor went home to bed.[1] Of the two stories Whitton's seems the more credible; as the Mayor does not attempt to assign any reason for the alleged riot.

Whitton also seems to have been continually annoying the Corporation with law suits; he had brought an action of Quo Warranto in the Queen's Bench; he had procured an action in the Exchequer against them for the arrears of the fee farm rent, and had commenced suits against them in the Courts of Star Chamber and Chancery.

With regard to the action for the arrears of the fee farm rent an exemplification of the record under the Great Seal is in the Borough Safe; and from it we learn that on 24th May, 1583, Sir John Popham, the Attorney General, laid an information before the Barons of the Exchequer that the fee farm rent of four marks yearly which had been reserved by the Charter of Henry VI had never been paid, and claiming the arrears amounting to £466 13s. 4d. The Mayor and Corporation did not appear for some time, and after their appearance the case was adjourned from term to term, till at length, in Hilary Term, 1588, the Attorney General entered a "nolle prosequi." When Skelton com-

[1] S.C.A.

E

plains of Whitton's action in procuring this suit in the
Exchequer he says that Whitton "well knew that the fee
farm rent hath been always by them paid to the hands of
the Lieutenant for the time being wherein they are to stand
. to her Majesty's grace and favour and to be relieved only by
humble petition to her, for that such payment to the hands of
her Lieutenant.is in extremity of law taken for no sufficient
discharge." And apparently such petition was presented to
the Queen, in consequence of which the Attorney General
dropped the case. The Lieutenant to whom the fee farm
had been paid was apparently the Lieutenant of the manor
and Park of Woodstock. Sir Henry Lee occupied that
office at this time, being also High Steward of the Borough,
and was accused by Whitton of retaining from him some of
the profits of his office; "the cause being that I made
known the concealing of four marks yearly which ought to
have been paid by the Mayor and Commonalty of Woodstock unto the Exchequer according to their patent."[m]

At last the patience of the Mayor and Commonalty was
exhausted; and in 1583 they presented a Bill of Complaint
against Whitton in the Court of Star Chamber reciting the
disturbances about Sterting Grove, and the occurrences
at the election of 1581, and on Palm Sunday. They also
charged him with misconduct when he was Mayor; they
alleged that during his year of office he received as forfeitures
and felons' goods a gelding with saddle and bridle worth
about £6, a case of rapiers worth twenty shillings, and other

[m] Cal. State Papers Eliz. 1580-1625, p. 26. This document is undated, but is calendared among the documents of 1580. This date is
probably incorrect, as the action in the Exchequer was not commenced
till 1583.

goods valued at about £20; and that "when former
Mayors had gently desired him to yield account" thereof,
"the said George Whitton hath in most outrageous sort
fallen out with them, calling them rebellious knaves, hell-
hounds, curre dogs, with divers other unmannerly terms
and names of contempt." But to this Whitton replied that
he certainly had received a "curtal horse of the value of
twenty shillings or thereabouts," and other things; but he
had out of them paid the fee farm rent, and had defended
suits brought against the Corporation for which the Council
had thanked him. He was also charged with having
obtained from the Mayor and Commonalty a grant of some
Borough property upon an undertaking that he would build
thereon and afterwards reconvey it to them, but that after
he had built a parlour and other buildings on the piece
of ground, he refused to reconvey it as he had agreed to
do. His reply was that his agreement had been to reconvey
a part only of the property, and that when he wished to do
so the Corporation would not accept the reconveyance.
There were other charges brought against him of malversa-
tion of the Borough Property, of deer stealing, and of usury;
but to these he returned an answer which at this distance of
time appears to be fairly adequate. These two latter
charges can only have been inserted with a view of
prejudicing Whitton in the eyes of the court, and thus
corroborate the views of those who prefer to consider these
disputes as a personal rather than a constitutional struggle.
Whitton's answer in the Star Chamber proceedings was
sworn on the 22nd November, 1583; we have already
noted the defences he made to the specific charges of the

Mayor, but his answer shows the struggle was still personal and not constitutional : he does not question the validity of the new orders ; he only expresses an opinion that the new order concerning the election of the Mayor is unwise, as it would keep the office among three men " being very unfit for the office " ; but apart from the Bill of Complaint and, the answer we have no further knowledge of the proceedings in the Star Chamber.

The next step in the struggle seems to have been taken by Whitton, who presented (probably to the Privy Council) a " supplication " which is now not to be found ; but as the Mayor appears to traverse every paragraph of the supplication seriatim we can form some idea of its contents. The first accusation against the Mayor was that " he with his con-federates by the name of a Common Council, a pack elected for that purpose, hath practised that there shall not be a new elected Mayor but himself to be chosen perpetually Mayor"; that Skelton was a victualler and did not adminster the assize of victuals ; and that he (Whitton) for standing in defence of the Charter was disfranchised by the Mayor and Common Council. The second charge appears to have been that the Mayor had wrongfully amerced Whitton and had com-menced an action at the Common Law to enforce the amercement ; then it was alleged that the Mayor had de-frauded the Queen of her moiety of the amercements levied during his Mayoralty ; and finally Whitton desired an order "of your Lordships" that the Mayor and Commonalty should discontinue all actions at the Common Law against him.

Skelton's answer to this supplication is preserved.[n] To

[n] S.A. See Note D.

the first charge he replied "that the Common Council . . . . hath been always used as a Common Council there, and are men of the best sort and most wise and discreet persons of the town"; and that when he had been Mayor he had "not continued year by year upon one only election but the same hath been laid upon him to his no small trouble and charge by such yearly nomination and election . . . . in which office he hath not (in the common opinion of the said town) been thought to be negligent to do his duty with the best services and endeavour he could."

He further answered that during his previous Mayoralties ("for that the wife of the said Skelton had beforetime used to make provision of diet . . . . for such resort as repaired thither at the time of market and on other such like occasions") he had sworn two men to keep the assize of bread and beer, and that since his last Mayoralty "there had not been made in his house any such provision otherwise than for his family"; and that Whitton had been disfranchised for "many contempts and misdemeanours and divers opprobrious and reproachful words to the Mayor for the time being." With regard to the second charge, the Mayor said that the reason why Whitton had been amerced was that he had set up certain pales in the High Street to the common nuisance : he pleaded that he was always ready to account to the Queen for her moiety of the amercements ; and that so far from the Mayor annoying Whitton with suits at the Common Law, there was then only pending the suit for the amercement,° but that on the other hand Whitton had

---

° This was perfectly correct ; proceedings in the Star Chamber were not suits at the Common Law.

commenced many actions against the Mayor and Commonalty (as we have previously seen). Unfortunately we do not know the result of Whitton's supplication ; for the Registers of the Privy Council contain no reference to these disturbances.[p]

So far the personal note in these troubles seems to have predominated ; but in 1584 we find the inhabitants petitioning Lord Burleigh the Lord High Treasurer, with a list of grievances " to be foreseen before the granting of the new Charter "; and in this petition the constitutional question becomes more prominent. There were many grounds of complaint which the petitioners desired should be corrected, but the principal complaint was that relating to the election of the Mayor, as follows :—

> " First, all inhabitants and tenants within the burgh of
> ancient time had and enjoyed divers great privileges
> and liberties by prescription before their said
> Charter, and by the said Charter every inhabitant
> and tenant is and ought to be free burgess. . . . . .
>
> " By the said Charter the election of the Mayor ought
> to be by the whole commonalty by common con-
> sent ; and also by letters of Privy Seal King
> Henry VII did strictly command and charge the
> town to make choice of the Mayor by general
> consent and such as were of good disposition, in-

---

[p] An entry in the Registers of the Acts of the Privy Council shows that other towns had similar troubles. At Doncaster, in 1589, two Mayors had been elected : one by the outgoing Mayor, the Aldermen, and the twenty-four "according to custom "; the other by the commonalty "according to the words of the charter." The two Mayors were summoned before the Privy Council, but the result is not recorded. (Registers, Privy Council, Eliz., vol. 8, p. 1004.)

differencie and sufficient ability. . . . . Furthermore
by the said Charter the Mayor of the town for the
time being hath the determination of all causes
concerning the assize of ale, bread and victuals.

" . . . . . But of late within these few years certain
victuallers of the same town being confederate
together, and having a Mayor for their purpose
who was also a victualler, have first brought to pass
contrary to their oath and charter that the Mayor
is yearly chosen by a few of their own pack and
confederates whom they name a Common Council,
and not by the voice of the commonalty, whereby
they assure themselves contrary to the ancient
statutes in this behalf evermore to elect a victualler
who will yearly for a fine certain dispense with all
victuallers to the utter decay of the poor." . . . . . .

They also allege that Skelton had illegally disfranchised
two Aldermen " only for maintaining their charter according
to their oaths "; and had levied illegal amercements; that
he had prohibited whom he listed from taking any benefit
in the meadow called " Le Pool," and " had restrained the
better sort from dealing in any manner touching the estate
of the town or employing of the common stock to the
public benefit of the town."

Although this petition was not signed by any of the
inhabitants of the Borough, Whitton's hand is clearly to be
recognized in it. The petitioners apply the same words to
the Common Council as had been used by Whitton a short
time previously; and the grounds of complaint so closely
resemble those referred to in Skelton's answer to Whitton's

supplication that this petition might be thought to be the document to which Skelton made answer; but as the petition contains no reference to the actions at the Common Law, this cannot be so.

The constitutional question referred to in the petition can at once be understood on reference to the orders of 1580. According to the petition all the inhabitants of the borough claimed to participate in the election of the Mayor and based their claims on the Charter of Henry VI ; we have seen that the new orders confined the franchise to the freemen, either because the latter were members of the Merchant Guild who had been so strong as to deprive the other inhabitants of the franchise ; or because the original grant was held to confer a personal and not a local franchise, and therefore did not confer the franchise on the immigrants since 1453 and their descendants who had not been admitted freemen of the town.[q] The petitioners do not seem to have objected to those orders which excluded them from any share in the trade of the town.

The complaint about the use of "Le Pool" seems to indicate that it had been common of pasture to all the burgesses till that date, and that thereafter it was let out to individuals who paid their rents to the Chamberlains. It has been so let since 1609 until this day, and, as we have seen, the accounts of 1518-9 show a sum of twenty shillings received in that year from the tenants of "Le Pool."

[q] The freemen did not necessarily reside within the Borough ; so that in some cases non-residents exercised their rights of a free burgess to the exclusion of the residents.

The Petition to Lord Burleigh was presented in view of the possible grant of a new Charter to the Borough, but such charter was never granted; nor have we any information of the way in which the various actions were finally settled. But the later history of the Borough shows us that although the freemen were unable to retain their privileges as members of the Merchant Guild—their monopoly of trading within the Borough—yet till the last they alone had the franchise, and maintained their superiority over the other inhabitants of the town. The scanty memoranda relating to the affairs of the Town during this period do not show that George Whitton was ever reinstated as an Alderman, but in 1587 he was acting as a Justice of the Peace for the Borough.

The occasion on which we find Whitton acting as a Justice of the Peace was on 6th February, 1587, when a return was made to the Privy Council of the quantity of corn that day in Woodstock. He had in his house, ten quarters of wheat and fifty-four quarters of barley and malt; but as his household consisted of sixteen persons, he was not ordered to send any to the market. Others did not fare so well; thus Nicholas Taylor who had forty quarters of barley and malt, and a household of only ten persons, was ordered "to furnish the market weekly thenceforth till Michaelmas with two bushels of barley and two bushels of malt": to ensure his obedience he was bound over in a recognizance of £4.[r] On the same day another return[s] was made of the Innholders and Victuallers in the town, with the quantity of malt they brewed weekly. There were four

[r] State Papers, Eliz., vol. 195, No. 25. [s] Ib., 26.

Innholders and eleven Victuallers; altogether sixty-one bushels of malt were brewed weekly in the town in varying quantities ranging from the twelve bushels brewed weekly by Kathcren Williams, Innholder, down to the single bushel brewed by John Bruce.[t] In view of the complaint contained in the petition to Lord Burleigh,[u] that the new provisions relating to the election of the Mayor had been carried by "certain victuallers confederate together," it is worthy of note that this list of innholders and victuallers contains the names of six out of the twenty-three members of the Council whose names are signed to the confirmation of the new orders in 1581, and that a seventh may possibly be the widow of one of the signatories.

While these disputes were being waged between the two factions in the town, a work was commenced of which the benefits are being felt at the present day. In 1585,[v] Richard Cornwell made his will by which he left £300 "to erect a free Grammar School for the town of New Woodstock where I was born; £100 for the house and £200 to purchase lands for the school and master, whom I would have to be a good preacher of the Word of God." To carry out these trusts the Mayor and Corporation, two years later, bought for £100 three houses situate in Oxford Street, one of which formerly belonged to the chantry of the Blessed Mary; and later, purchased an annuity or

---

[t] John Bruce was then Sergeant-at-Mace; and it appears that one of the houses belonging to the Town was known as the Sergeant's house, and was licensed for the sale of intoxicating liquors. When in the eighteenth century the Town paid for beer for distribution, some of it was always given away at the Sergeant's house.

[u] C.C.   [v] Charity Reports, 1819-35.   Oxfordshire, p. 49.

rent charge of £8 arising from lands at Childrey, Bucks. The school for centuries was held in a long room which ran parallel to the Chancel of St. Mary's Church, and was said to have been given to the Corporation by Queen Elizabeth as part of the Chantry of the Blessed Mary; and the Master received the rents of these houses and the proceeds of the rent charge as his stipend. At the present time the school is held in one of the three houses above referred to, and the stipend is accordingly reduced.

THE MARKET-PLACE.

(Showing the sign of the " Bear " Hotel, and the present Post Office.)

CHAPTER V.

Social Life before the Civil War.

IN our third chapter we studied the constitution under which the inhabitants of Woodstock were governed during the first half of the seventeenth century; let us now try to picture to ourselves how this constitution worked in practice, and how the social life of two hundred and fifty years ago differed from that of to-day. We have splendid material to enable us to compile this picture, in the Chamberlains' accounts from 1609 to 1650, and the Book of the Acts of the Portmouth Court from 1622 to 1635; unfortunately the extant books of the Acts of the Council do not commence before 1651.

When the well-known Dr. Mavor (of spelling-book fame) was Mayor of the Borough in the early years of this century he collected from the loose records of the Views of Frankpledge many lists of the inhabitants of the Borough at various times; the list returned to the View of Frankpledge at Michaelmas 1627 shows that there were then in the town twenty-three members of the Council, forty-five freemen, forty-three inhabitants not freemen, and thirteen widows : a total of 124 families at the most; an average of five persons to a family would give 620 inhabitants.   A list in the Acts of the Council for 28th August, 1662, gives the names of twenty-four members of the Council, fifty-eight freemen, fifty-six inhabitants not freemen, and eight widows —146 families or 730 inhabitants.   In 1635 only seventy persons were assessed to the Ship Money ; but the orders from the Privy Council to the Mayor empowered him to exempt the very poor from the payment of this tax. Twenty-one freeholders of the borough were summoned to Oxford in 1625 to vote for Knights of the shire.

The relative importance of the town at this time is best ascertained by a glance at the documents in the Borough Records relating to Ship Money.

When the tax was first levied in 1635 the County of Oxford was ordered to furnish one ship of 350 tons burthen, and manned by a crew of 140 men, or in default to pay a sum of £3,500.   This amount was apportioned by the High Sheriff among the hundreds and towns of the county ; the assessments on the towns were as follows[a] :—

---

[a] These figures should be compared with the following, which show the annual rateable values of the same towns in 1890, as given in

Oxford	... ...	£100
Henley	... ...	£ 60
Banbury	... ...	£ 40
Chipping Norton	...	£ 30
Burford	... ...	£ 40
Woodstock	... ...	£ 20

The actual sum raised by the Borough of New Woodstock was £20 2s. 2d., and it is noteworthy that considerably more than half of this amount was borne by eight persons only. The Mayor, Mr. William Meatcalfe, was assessed at £1 10s., and four Aldermen, the Town Clerk, and two Gentlemen were assessed at £1 6s. 8d. each, a total of £10 16s. to be paid by these eight alone; seven persons were assessed at one shilling each, and the others paid sums varying from eight shillings to two shillings. There does not appear to have been much demur on the part of the inhabitants of Woodstock to the payment of this tax; as on the assessment is an endorsement in the handwriting of Mr. Edmund Hiorne the Town Clerk that "This money within mentioned was paid by Mr. Rayer to Mr. French the undersheriff at Mr. Carter's house in Oxon within a month after this assessment."

When the second levy for Ship Money was made in December, 1636, the assessment of Woodstock was reduced to £15; but this time the tax was not collected without difficulty; for in the next March the High Sheriff of the

Kelly's Directory for 1891 :—Oxford, £215,539; Henley, £16,386; Banbury, £20,054; Chipping Norton, £11,259; Burford, £3,042; and Woodstock, £2,979. But it must be remembered that some of these Boroughs have enlarged their boundaries since the seventeenth century.

County wrote to Secretary Nicholas that Banbury, Woodstock, Chipping Norton, and Burford were backward with
their Ship Money.[b] Except the writ there is no document
in the Borough Safe relating to this second levy.

The Book of Acts of the Portmouth Court contains few
records of what we should to-day consider as Police cases;
there are a number of examinations of witnesses relating to
various offences; but there are few records of the punishments that were inflicted; in most cases the offenders were
bound over to appear at the Sessions, and then we lose sight
of them. It appears, however, that in a number of cases
those who had done wrong were compelled to enter into
recognizances with sureties not to so offend again; and if
punishments are designed to prevent a recurrence of crime,
this method of procedure seems fully to meet the case; for
not only would the offender be careful to keep within the
bounds of right so as to prevent his goods being seized
under the recognizance, but his two sureties would check
his misbehaviour so that they too might be saved harmless.
It is possible, however, that many persons were punished
summarily, and no record kept of the punishments; there
are frequent entries in the Chamberlains' accounts of payments for the repair of the pillory, the stocks, the cucking
stool and the cage. In 1620 the cucking stool was thoroughly
repaired, as appears by the following extract from the
accounts :—

"Paid to Symonds for squaring a peece of tymber to
make the coocking stoole 6*d*. Item, for the same peece
of tymber beinge 21 foote in length 4*s*. Item, paid for

[b] Calendar State Papers, 1636-7, p. 494.

oaken tymber to make the chaier and for nayles 19*d*. Item for sawinge the same peece 6*d*. Itm to Symons and his man for one dayes work and a halfe with 3*d*. in beere 3*s*."

But in spite of its repair the only evidence that it was ever used is that on 17th April, 1675, the View of Frankpledge ordered Sarah Heathen to be ducked as she had confessed and admitted being a disturber of the peace. A new pair of gyves was purchased in 1609 for 2*s*.

In 1629 the magistrates ordered George Chambers (who had confessed to being drunk and disorderly) to pay 3*s*. 6*d*. " to be given to the poor of Woodstock to pray for him to amend the course of his life."

During the fourteen years for which the records remain (1622-1635) there does not appear to have been much serious crime in Woodstock ; apart from drunkenness and quarrelling the chief vice of the inhabitants seems to have been sheep-stealing—a vice which was far more prevalent in those days than now. In the year 1625 the Mayor heard three separate charges of sheep-stealing, and committed the accused to the assizes in each case ; we do not know what happened to them there, but the probability is that they were hanged. Only one case of poaching is recorded : on 3rd November, 1625, nine men confess to have stolen eleven conies from the woods of Sir Henry Lee, but they are not punished ; they are merely enjoined not to offend Sir Henry Lee again. A more serious matter had been brought before the Mayor a few weeks previously ; for Edward Hall, a tailor of Oxford, was accused of having said, in the public-house kept by Thomas Godfrey, "that there was a King newly proclaimed in Scotland." His

Worship evidently considered these words to be treasonable, for he committed Hall to the Assizes and reported the matter to the Privy Council, but neither in this case do we know the result.

At this time vagrancy was punished far more strictly than it is to-day. A century earlier, "valiant and sturdy beggars" refusing to work were to be punished by whipping for the first offence, loss of an ear for the second, and hanging for the third (27 Hen. VIII, c. 25).

On 27th October, 1624, a woman named "Chester, late of Westminster, late servant with William Lange, of Tuttle Street, Cooper, taken here as a masterless person without any habitation remaining here since August last was punished according to the Statute, and was sent to Britton, in Somersetshire, to her father, John Chester, a shoemaker there."

Labourers who desired to go on lawful business from one part of the country to another were furnished with passes by the Justices ; such passes were frequently forged : e.g., on 9th October, 1634, William Faux, William Edwards, and Elizabeth his wife, were taken before the Justices at Woodstock, " being all vagrants wandering with counterfeit passes and seals upon them, and were taken drunk yesterday." It was ordered that they be well " whipped and sent with several passes to their late habitations, and their seals to be taken from them." Faux was given a pass to Launceston in Cornwall.

But in those days as to-day there were many duties that devolved upon the magistrates other than the administration of justice : the Justices were the licensing authority, and

F

seem to have been most liberal in granting licences. For while the population of the Borough was under 750, yet in the years between 1618 and 1635 the number of licensed houses varied between fourteen and twenty-six. On 20th March, 1623, the Mayor reported to the Privy Council that he had suppressed all needless alehouses, and reformed the immoderate strength of beer[c]; yet eleven days later fifteen taverns and alehouses were licensed,—in other words at least one alehouse to every fifty of the population of the town. Every innkeeper was bound over in recognizances of £10, with two sureties in £5 each, to observe the regulations laid down by the magistrates and the King's proclamations; he was not to allow gambling, nor to allow any person to remain in his house above a day and a night without delivering his true name to the constables of the Borough; he must close at nine o'clock in the evening and during service time on Sundays and holy days; he must observe the Assize of Bread and Beer; and in 1619 he was bound not to "utter nor willingly suffer to be uttered, drunk, taken or tippled any tobacco within his said house, shop, cellar, or other place thereunto belonging."

Those who victualled without licence were fined, and obliged to procure sureties not to so offend again.

Moreover, for some years at the beginning of Lent the magistrates compelled the Licensed Victuallers and the Butchers of the town to enter into bonds with two sureties each not to "dress any flesh in their houses during this Lent time, nor upon any Friday or Saturday, nor upon the Ember Days, nor upon any other days called vigils, nor

[c] Cal. S.P., 1619-23, p. 532.

upon any other days commonly called fish days, nor at any other times prohibited for any respect, nor to suffer it to be eaten contrary to the law." To ascertain whether these conditions had been observed it was usual to empanel a jury "to enquire of the killing, eating, and dressing of flesh." In February, 1623-4, John Durbridge confessed to the jury to have eaten flesh in his house this Lent, and was fined 12d.; and a similar fine was imposed on six others who had committed the same offence; while Richard Cole, a butcher, was fined 10s. for dressing and selling flesh during Lent. After 1629, the jury still presented the offenders, but no fines seem to have been imposed.

Another duty devolving upon the Mayor was the holding of the Assize of Bread and Beer, when he fixed the prices at which all the brewers, bakers, and victuallers within the Borough were to sell these commodities. At these times a jury was empanelled whose duty it was to ascertain the prices of the various qualities of wheat and malt on the previous market day; and in accordance with their finding the Mayor fixed the price of beer and the weights of the penny loaves according to their quality.

Thus when the best wheat was sold at 40s. a quarter and the second quality at 36s. (as on the 14th September, 1623), the penny white loaf was to weigh 8 oz. 4 dwt.; the penny wheaten loaf, 12 oz. 12 dwt.; and the penny household loaf, 16 oz. 18 dwt. On the same date the best malt was sold at 33s. 4d. a quarter, and the Mayor fixed the price of the strongest beer at 9s. 6d. a barrel. But whatever the price of a barrel of strong beer might be, the Mayor always ordered every Innholder to sell a quart for one penny, and two quarts of small drink for one penny. The bakers did not always observe these orders, and were often presented by the jury at the next assize for their disobedience. On 6th September, 1626, Christopher Smith was presented "because he divers times did want two and three ounces of his bread after the last assize," and he was therefore fined 13s. 4d.[d]

A little earlier in the seventeenth century the Mayor held the Assize, not only for bread and beer but for all victuals; the only record of such an assize is that dated 20th August, 1604, and the prices of everything differed so much from those of the present day that a somewhat lengthy list may be interesting :—

A pound of butter	$2\frac{1}{2}d.$
Ten eggs, the best in the market ...	2d.
A stone of best beef weighing 8 lbs. ...	14d.
A quarter of best mutton	2s. 0d.
A fat goose, the best in the market ...	10d.
A fat pig, ditto	16d.
A couple of chicken or rabbits, ditto ...	13d.
A dozen pigeons, ditto	10d.
A pound of tallow candles	3d.
A hundredweight of sweet hay ...	12d.
A hundred good faggots, with carriage ...	3s. 8d.
A thousand bricks	10s. 0d.
A quarter of charcoal, being 8 bushels ...	14d.

The prices to be charged by the Licensed Victuallers of the town were settled at this assize : one penny was the legal charge for a feather bed for one man for one night,

[d] For a copy of the Assize, see Appendix B.

while if he stayed for a week he was to pay sixpence ; if, however, he preferred to share a mattress or a flock bed with another man the charge was to be fourpence'a week. If six or more had dinner or supper together and had "good bread and drink, beef or mutton boiled or roast . . . or otherwise upon the fish days having good bread and drink, salt fish, or salt salmon, herring, egg and butter. . . ." each was to pay sixpence ; while hay and litter day and night for one horse in every inn cost fivepence, and fourpence was the legal charge for a vacant or empty chamber or stable by the week.

Within a few days of the holding of the Assize of Bread all the weights and measures in the town were brought to the Mayor, and by him compared with the standards kept in the Guild Hall, and allowed or disallowed accordingly ; the standard bushel procured in 1670 is still preserved in the Council Chamber. In 1624 the Chamberlains paid two shillings for a new market bushel, and in 1645 for one bound with iron and chains they paid eight shillings ; and in 1611 "a seale to seale potts and waights" cost three shillings and fourpence. Although the Statute of Apprentices was still unrepealed in the seventeenth century, by which the magistrates were empowered to fix the daily wages of labourers within their jurisdiction, yet the Borough records afford no evidence that the Justices ever fixed the legal rate of wages at Woodstock.

We have already noticed that the hearing of many offences was adjourned by the magistrates to the Sessions, when the matter was finally decided by a full bench among whom the Recorder always sat; but other business was always transacted on that day in addition to the administration of justice, for then was held the town's meeting known as the View of Frankpledge.   In fact, the records never appear to make any distinction between the business of the Sessions and that of the View of Frankpledge, for the heading of the notes of the day's business is always, "Sessio pacis ac etiam visus franci plegii" (Session of the Peace and also View of Frankpledge).   Centuries before this time the Frankpledge was an institution by which all the men of a town or village became sureties for one another's honesty ; and even at Woodstock in the seventeenth century we find some slight traces of its original intention.   For on 5th April, 1632, at the View of Frankpledge, "George Gregorie was ordered to enter into sufficient bonds with sureties of £40 within a fortnight to save the Town harmless from his new tenant Richard Taylor"; presumably he was to guarantee that Taylor should never become chargeable to the town as a pauper : and there are several other orders to a like effect.

The name "View of Frankpledge" was given to that institution, which in other towns was known as the Court Leet (although these latter words are never used in the Woodstock Records) and was technically a Court of Justice to inquire into nuisances and offences, *e.g.*, whether the officers had done their duties, whether the roads had been repaired, whether false weights or measures had been used, whether the pound had been broken open, &c., &c.[e] But in practice it was a democratic town's meeting at which all the inhabitants were obliged to appear,

[e] See Charge to Jury in Notes on History of Chipping Norton, p. 36.

and every one had a right to speak. The Mayor presided, having some days previously issued his precept to the Sergeant-at-Mace to summon certain of the inhabitants to serve as jurors and the remainder, whether freemen or not, to attend the Court; any person whatever could lodge a complaint before the jury. After the jury had been sworn they proceeded to elect two constables, four tything men (who acted as assistant constables), and two ale-tasters, who held their various offices for a year. Service was obligatory on those who were elected; thus in 1629 Robert Brun was fined forty shillings for refusing to take upon him the office of ale-taster. At Chipping Norton, within the memory of many now living, the jury of the Court Leet inspected the town after they had been sworn, and presented those who had created nuisances or offended against the bye-laws of the Borough. There were no bye-laws at Woodstock, but the jury made occasional orders for the good of the town. Thus on 26th October, 1625, the View of Frankpledge ordered that no man thereafter should lay any muck out of his house in the common street upon pain of five shillings. And on an odd sheet, which apparently belonged to an older book of Acts of the Portmouth Court, is part of the Record of the View of Frankpledge held in October, 1580, from which it appears that the jury made an order " That no glover dwellinge within this towne shall from hence forth have above twoe buyers uppon any markett or fayer daye, and that no foren glover shall have anye buyer but himself or one for him, and non of them shall buye anye fell or fells before they be brought into the markett place appointed for the same (that is to saye) betwene the corner of Richard

Lowe's house, the markett stone pitched against the Guild
Hall unto the upper ende of Crown Lane, uppon payne to
forfett for every offence to the contrarye iiis. iiiid."[1]   Not
only did the jury make orders, but they presented and
punished all who caused nuisances.   On the back of one of
the undated lists of the inhabitants is one series of presentments : William Bradshaw and two others were presented
and fined fourpence each for casting their fishwater into the
street, and Jerram White was fined twopence for keeping
his hogs unringed.

The jury had occasionally to settle disputes about property.   In 1626 William Seares and his mother (who had
married a second time) could not agree as to the dower
to which she was entitled in the house which he had
inherited from his father ; and the jury presented " the
thirds belonging to her to be the rooms following, viz.,
the hall, the old buttery, and the third part of the back
side next to John Archer's as it is stoned out by the
jury " ; and in the next year they decided which of two
adjoining owners should repair the fence between their
properties.   In 1631 Thomas Horne, of Oxford, labourer,
was convicted on his own confession of being a forestaller
(i.e., of buying goods before they had been brought to
market), and was committed to prison.   In 1580 Alice
Norman, widow, was presented for selling unsound meat,
for which she was fined twopence.

The two ale-tasters had probably been the informants in
these two cases, for it was their duty to enforce the market
regulations.   They not only had to be on their guard

[1] See Appendix C.

against forestalling, regrating (*i.e.*, buying to sell again in the same market) and engrossing (*i.e.*, buying up small quantities of goods by retail in order to sell wholesale), but they had to enforce the statute concerning the sale of leather[r]; this was very stringent, and provided for the appointment of an official who was to examine all leather exposed for sale, and seize such as was improperly tanned. On 26th September, 1625, John Doa, the taster, seized nine bundles and a half of tanned leather belonging to Mr. Thomas Wilks, of Chipping Norton, because they were unlawfully tanned; Wilks was fined four shillings "for selling leather unsealed contrary to the statute," and the leather was declared to be forfeited to the King. In 1622 John Viall received twopence "for making a new seal to seal leather with."

For some reason or other one of the constables was sent to Blackheath to train in 1615, and his expenses (12*s.*) were paid by the town. At the previous Christmas he and his colleague had taken charge of the town armour, which consisted of :—

" Itm, twoe cosletts furnished remayning in the hall.

Itm, ii calliners furnisshed.

Itm, one muskett furnisshed without flaske and tutchbox.

Itm, three swords and three daggers on lether belts.

Itm, two headpees and one Fack for a horstrion without sleeves.

Itm, pike newe bought and one ould pike in the ball.

Itm, Wm. Raunson hath one dagger in his house."

[r] 1 Jac. I., c. 22.

A "flask and tutchbox" were forthwith bought for the musket at the price of twelvepence.

The last two items of information are taken from the book of Chamberlains' accounts, which are preserved in great detail, and are full of a variety of information. The annual income of the town during the period under review rose gradually from £50 to £100 a year, and usually the expenditure was a few pounds higher than the income. An abstract of the accounts for the financial year 1624-5 is as follows :—

RECEIPTS.

	£	s.	d.
Rents	24	18	10¼
Market Tolls	11	14	5¾
Rent of the Wool Beam ...	1	4	0
Admissions	2	6	8
Encroachment	1	0	0
Fines for misdeeds	0	19	0
Fines paid by foreign bakers for permission to sell in the town	0	14	0
Grammar School Endowment ...	13	0	0
	£55	17	0

EXPENDITURE.

	£	s.	d.
Christmas Gifts	4	19	4
Paid to messengers for bringing Royal proclamations* ...	3	2	0

* In 1626 the messenger agreed to receive 13s. 4d. a year as a composition for his fees when he brought the proclamations.

Paid in wine	...	...	2 8 1
Salaries	...	...	28 11 8
Fee farm and Chantry Rents	...	8 2 0
Given to poor people	...	1 5 2
Expenses at the King's visit	...	2 17 10
Repairs, &c.	...	...	1 16 3
Renewing the Commission of the Peace	...	...	...	2 4 6
Sundries	...	...	...	1 19 11½

£57 6 9½

A glance at this abstract will show that then as now the property given to the Town by Henry VI and Queen Elizabeth formed the mainstay of the Borough Finances; the rents, which in 1609 amounted only to £27 2s. 7d., rose in 1649 to £53 2s. 8d. The Corporation Meadows, which are now let for almost £100 a year, in 1608 brought in only £13 13s. 4d.; and for a house then let at £1 6s. 8d. the tenant now pays £18 a year. When the town was in need of money it sold certain of its property to pay its debts; thus in 1618 Mr. Edmond Hiorne, the Town Clerk, purchased the fee farm of his dwelling-house next the Church for a sum of £30 in cash, and the old rent of ten shillings a year; and at the same time he gave £13 for the fee farm of two other houses.[h]

[h] The deed conveying these houses to Mr. Hiorne is among the deeds in the Borough Safe. The house wherein he dwelt stood between the North side of the Church and the High Street, and was bounded East and West by two passages leading to the Church; but the Mayor and Commonalty reserved to themselves " the nether room with the chamber over the same next unto the north door of . . .

As the greater part of the town property consisted of houses, a large proportion of the income had to be expended in repairs ; and it should be noticed that in all these repairs the Chamberlains seem to have dealt directly with the labourers who were employed, and to have themselves purchased the materials and superintended the works. In no case during the forty-two years between 1609 and 1650 do we find that any contractor was employed, except for minor works, such as cleansing the town gutters and the like. The largest work which was undertaken during this period was the erection of an almshouse in 1612 at a total charge of £32 0s. 1d., which included a sum of two shillings and sixpence which was paid for the demolition of the old building. Unskilled labourers for digging stone in the church-yard received tenpence a day. Warren the mason and the carpenter were each paid one shilling a day, and their boys eightpence a day ; while 6,000 slates cost £3. The whole account is set out item by item, and is well worth the study of any'one interested in the social life of the times. Thatchers' wages in 1610 were tenpence a day, and lime in 1611 was tenpence a bushel. In 1616 the expenses incurred in repairing the dial and cross amounted. to £4 3s. 8d., including a sum of six shillings spent "for a drinking upon the free mason and John Cooper when they first came to see the dial." Thirty-three pounds of sheet lead were used in this work, at a cost of twopence a pound. Glass was fivepence halfpenny a foot in 1619, and that same

and adjoining the said Church," which was used as the Town Clerk's office. The other two houses were on the other side of Park Street, but the descriptions are insufficient for identification.

year stone was brought into the town from Handborough Quarry at a cost of two shillings a load ; in the next year three new ladders were purchased for the town at a cost of fourteen shillings and eightpence. In 1622 some of the streets of the town were pitched at twopence a yard ; and in 1630 the Chamberlains mowed the meadow at Hampton Poyle, which was unlet, and paid ninepence a day to the men and fivepence a day to the women whom they employed. In 1631 the· draw-well in Oxford Street was new made at a cost of £4 15s. 11d. ; and in 1627 expenses amounting to eleven shillings and eightpence were incurred in "new making the Bench about the Great Elm in Oxford Street."

That the town should spend £2 8s. 1d. in wine during a single year requires explanation : some of it was set before the Justices at the Sessions and the Assessment of the Subsidies, and on other occasions. But there are no less than twenty-two entries, of which the following may be taken as a type :—" For a quart of sack to Mr. Evans when he preached and dyned at Mr. Maiors, 12d." The cost of the wine given to the preachers during this year (1624-5) amounted to £1 15s. 1d.

Occasionally the King or the Prince or members of the nobility who resided near the Town sent a present of venison to the Corporation, and the expense of cooking such vension was always defrayed out of the Corporation income. Thus in 1611 £6 17s. was paid "for expenses in eating the two bucks which the Prince bestowed on the Town"; of this over £4 was spent in wine ; and among the other items of expense were two bushels of wheat at four

shillings a bushel, ten pounds of suet at fourpence a
pound, two pounds of pepper at two shillings and sixpence a pound, and fourteen pounds of butter at fourpence
a pound.

But the Common Fund was often employed to better
purposes. We have seen that in 1625 the Mayor ordered
£1 5s. 2d. (about two·per cent. of the Borough income)
to be given to poor persons living in the Town.   In
1615 sixpence was paid "for the making of two smocks
for Joan and Ann Cope of an old sheet"; in the next year
two shrouds were procured for "goodwife Gilbert and
Roger Norwood" at a cost of four shillings and sixpence.
In 1611 two shirts for a poor boy at the Almshouse cost
two shillings; and twenty years later three yards and a half
of blue cloth to make a coat for Lucas, the Beadle of the
beggars, cost ten shillings and sixpence.   Then, as now,
there was distress in Ireland, and in 1631 the Mayor gave
twelvepence to five Irish gentlewomen, who presumably
were on tramp, and at the same time one poor scholar
received sixpence.   Nor was the Mayor's charity confined
to the inhabitants of the town, for on 24th December, 1613,
five shillings were given to the town of Bicester towards the
new erecting of burned houses; and on 14th December,
1641, two shillings were given to "three poor men of Witney
that had their houses burned . . . . that they should not beg
the town."   An entry of a somewhat similar nature occurs
in 1631, when sixpence was "given to a poor woman that
would have lyen-in in the town, to get her away."

In 1646 eighteen shillings were given to " Goodwife
Richardson for wages for keeping the sick people"; and

Francis Richardson received fourteen shillings "for watching about sick people's doors."

It was the custom of the town to present Christmas gifts to the neighbouring gentry ; for instance, at Christmas, 1624, Sir Gerard Fleetwood, Knight, was the recipient of a cake costing ten shillings, and a sugar loaf weighing seven pounds, costing nine and fourpence ; and when the Corporation waited on him with the gift they distributed six shillings in rewards to his servants.   At the same they gave a similar cake to Sir Henry Browne (of Kiddington), and eleven shillings to his servants.   Sir Henry Lee, of Ditchley, received a cake and sugar loaf like those presented to Sir Gerard Fleetwood, and his servants received twenty-three shillings ; while to Mr. Parson Browne was presented a sugar loaf weighing eight pounds, and costing ten shillings and eightpence.

There are a number of curious entries set out in the Chamberlains' accounts which deserve some slight notice ; perhaps the most curious payment is one in 1634 :—

> " Paied for expenses upon fouer witches that were sent from London to go into Lanke-sheir by the Kings appointmt at the Coontries chardge which is to be allowed back to the Town at the next Quarter Sessions after Xmas 1634, as by the particular bill thereof appeareth   ...   ...   23*s.* "

But no repayment of this amount appears in the accounts for the next year.

Another entry foreshadows the Municipal Band of the London County Council of to-day.   The Mayor ordered three shillings and twopence to be paid "for music at the bringing home of the elm from Combe on May Day, 1610, as a Maypole."

John Aubrey notes a curious custom at Woodstock in his time, *viz.*, that the young people of the town were wont to go into the Park on May Day and gather hawthorn which they set up before their houses, and to finish the day with music and dancing; and within the memory of many now living the Maypole was set up at Whitsuntide on the green opposite the railway station, and a dancing booth called "My Lady's Bower" was there built of green boughs, which would hold a large number of people. A refreshment booth was erected in a garden where the Police Station now stands; over the door was fixed a cage, containing a pair of owls, which were referred to as "my lady's parrots," and over the cage a pair of flails, which were likewise called "my lord's nut-crackers"; there was also a wooden horse which was called "my lady's palfrey"; and any one who miscalled either the owls, the flails, or the horse was fined a quart of ale. The last Queen of the Revels is still living; as are a few of the Morris dancers. In 1614 there was "given to Ellinor Collins, our Whitsuntide lady, one apron cloth by Mr. Mayor's appointment"; but the receipts from the Whitsun Ale, which in 1609 amounted to £7 1s. 6d., went for very many years to defray the church expenses.

On 11th February, 1614-15, "the towne did give out of thaire stock £5 to the King's Majesty for a gratuity by means of a letter written to the Maior and Commonalty from the Privy Council, and was paid to Sir Thomas

a Centrum phonocampticum.
b Centrum phonicum.
c Chaucer's house.
d the Rivulet.
e Wood Rock.

DR. PLOT'S VIEW OF THE MANOR HOUSE.

Spencer, Knight, one of the collectors thereof for the
County of Oxford." In 1631 sixpence was paid "for a
little book of orders and directions to the Justices concerning corn buyers and sellers," and in 1638 two pence were
"paid to Duke to go to Wootton to inform the town of
Wootton to prevent the coming of one suspected to be sick
of the plague."

The receipts include entries which differ widely from
those found in municipal accounts of the present day. All
waifs and strays belonged to the town ; thus in 1631 John
Meades paid ten shillings for a stray bullock, and in 1636
£2 10s. was received "for a sorrel gelding sold by the
town that was a waif." Felons' goods also fell to the town.
Scriptural reminiscences are revived when we read that in
1609 the town received ten shillings for "one cloak taken
from the Egyptians." In 1617 the town received eighteenpence of John Pepper for a pair of stolen shoes. In the
accounts for 1630 is the following entry :—

"Received for wool sold that was taken upon Andrew
    Homes a convicted felon eleven shillings, besides
    ten shillings in money of his remaining in the hands
    of James Nicholls, late constable."

As we have noticed in the abstract of the accounts
for the year 1625, all the fines for offences against the laws
either of the realm or of the town were paid to the
Chamberlains.

King James and his court often visited Woodstock Manor
for the sake of the hunting ; and Hearne has copied the
inscriptions affixed to sundry antlers at Ditchley House
recording in somewhat halting verse the quality of the sport

afforded the King before he became possessed of the trophies.[1] There is a tradition that one stag in either this reign or the next led the chase to Stokenchurch in Bucks, a distance of over twenty miles as the crow flies. But it was not only the Court that hunted at Woodstock; for on 22nd October, 1627, Charles I wrote to the Earl of Pembroke, then Chancellor of the University of Oxford, that he had just cause to be displeased at the presumption taken by the Scholars of Oxford in killing his game at Woodstock, and ordering the Vice-Chancellor to assemble the heads of the colleges and expel such as were guilty from the University, and inflict such further punishment as the nature of their offence should require.[J]

We have already noted the fact that in 1625 the Corporation treated the preachers to wine on no less than twenty-two occasions; in 1616 they gave wine to the preachers on sixteen occasions, in 1618 on nineteen, in 1631 on twenty-six, and in 1639 on twenty-three. It will be remembered that one of the orders of 1580 prescribed that the Corporation should accompany the Mayor to church every day when there was any preaching or sermon. The Rector of the parish resided at Bladon, two miles away; what was more natural than that wine should be given him after each sermon? If, as is probable, the town paid for wine for the preacher every time there was a sermon, the entries in the Chamberlains' accounts will show the number of times in each year when sermons were preached. Now after 1623 the Corporation paid for five sermons preached in the Church at Woodstock on certain days from a fund derived

---

[1] Marshall, p. 173.   [J] Calendar State Papers, 1626-7, p. 402.

under the will of Aldermen Fletcher, and they were paying
for these sermons in 1625. Take five from twenty-two and
seventeen remain ; we may therefore presume that these
remaining seventeen sermons represented the ordinary
sermons of the Rector of Bladon in Woodstock Church ;
in other words, that sermons were preached only on every
third Sunday. The number of payments in other years
favours this presumption, and further shows that the Rector
was not over particular as to one or two, more or less, in
any year. In corroboration of this presumption we may
quote from the Court Book of the Archdeaconry of Oxford,
which records that on 28th December, 1633, Martin
Royse, Curate of Bladon, was cited before the Archdeacon
of Oxford, and personally made answer "that there are
sermons preached by this respondent for the most part
every third Sunday, but he confesseth that in harvest time
last there was not a sermon preached in six weeks."[k]

The book of Churchwardens' accounts, which begins with
the year 1613, shows that in that year their receipts came
to £12 10s. 11d., and their disbursements to £13 13s. 6d. ;
and of the balance, nineteen shillings were due to Mr. Rayer
for wine (presumably for the Communion). The church
goods then delivered to the new Churchwardens included
a velvet pall, a fustian pall, a surplice, "a silver cup for the
Communion with a cover of silver and a napkin to wrap the
cup in, a Bible, two books of Common Prayers in folio,
one Psalter in quarto, one book of Homilies, two books of
Articles, and one book of Canon Laws." In 1620 the
old Bible was sold for ten shillings, and a new one bought

[k] Marshall, p. 297.

for forty-four shillings. Later, at a Vestry Meeting held in the Church on Sunday, June 2nd, 1633, it was agreed that every communicant should give a halfpenny to the Clerk in payment for the Bread and Wine.

OLD HOUSE, 1697.

CHAPTER VI.

The Civil War and After.

WHILE the documents for the first forty years of
the seventeenth century throw light mainly on
the social and economic life of the Borough,
those for the remainder of the century, consisting only of
Acts of the Council and Proceedings in the Portmouth
Court, principally deal with the municipal and political life
of the Burgesses.

Owing to its proximity to the King's head-quarters at
Oxford, Woodstock saw more of the military forces on
both sides than many places of ten times its size and
wealth. The Manor House was quickly garrisoned by the
Royal troops and put into a fit state of defence; the ruins

oɪ Rosamund's Bower, of which walls and pillars twenty feet high had remained till that time, were destroyed in order that they might not give shelter to any who might wish to attack the Manor House.[a] The burgesses were divided : William Lenthall, the well-known Speaker of the Long Parliament, was one of their representatives ; but Edmund Hiorne, the Town Clerk, had already given the town armour to the Royalist party,[b] and had posted up the proclamation denouncing the Earl of Essex as a traitor ; the Chamberlains' accounts show that sixpence was expended in beer "when the muskets were spoken for," and that a man was paid fourpence to watch the pro-clamation against the Earl of Essex. On 4th October, 1642, Hiorne was summoned to appear on his knees at the Bar of the House of Commons for his share in this business, and "Mr. Speaker declared unto him the nature of his offence, which was very heinous ; and he did . . . . humbly acknowledge his offence and was heartily sorry for it." After the indecisive battle of Edge Hill on 23rd October, 1642, the King stayed one night at the Manor House on his way back to Oxford, and the Mayor then gave twenty shillings in cash to the King's and Prince's footmen, and five shillings and sixpence to their trumpeters. Im-mediately following the entries of these payments are two that appear to be closely connected with them :—

"To a girl to go to Kidlington ...   ...   6d.
To John Norman, to go as a guide in the
    night to Charlbury   ...   .   1s."

[a] John Aubrey's MS. Notes in Plot's Oxfordshire, in Bodleian Library (Ashm., 1722). See view of Manor House on page 1.
[b] Journal H. C., ii, 792.

It is probable that at least two Woodstock men served in the Royal army, and came back safe from the field of Edge Hill; for on 26th October, 1642, the Chamberlains paid one pound to Edward Silver and William Drinkwater, "trained soldiers for their charge."

Nothing much seems to have occurred at Woodstock except occasional visits of troops and of their Majesties, till on 17th June, 1644, the Manor House was captured by the Parliamentary forces under Sir William Waller, who thus reports his proceedings to the Committee of both Kingdoms.[c]

"I marched to Woodstock, where the enemy the day before had put in some musketeers under the command of Captain Foster, an officer of the Earl of Lindsay's. Some troops of our horse drawing up about the house to lay the passages till the foot came up, one of our horsemen rode up to the gate and called to speak with the Captain, who very unwisely came out upon the soldier's bare word, and he very fairly when the Captain would have returned disarmed him and took him prisoner. Those within, as soon as I came, upon assurance of quarter from me, yielded themselves prisoners."

However, the Royalist forces appear to have soon regained their old position, for on the 2nd November in the same year, the Royal foot were reported to be at Woodstock with six pieces of ordnance;[d] and in spite of an assault by Colonel Fleetwood in February, 1645, they appear to have held the place till May 8th, when the King and Queen

[c] Calendar State Papers, 1644, p. 363.   [d] Ib., 1644-5, p. 90.

and their troops marched to Stow-on-the-Wold.[e] They evacuated the position only just in time, for Cromwell was in the town four days later with five hundred horse and foot, and thence went on to Islip.[f] It is probable that Cromwell's was only a flying visit, and that he did not leave a garrison ; for we find that in October, 1645, Woodstock was in possession of the Royal forces, who continued to hold the Manor House till 26th April, 1646, when it was surrendered by Captain Fawcett after twenty days' siege,[g] during which it had been severely battered about. The following day King Charles left Oxford on his way to the Scots army at Newark.

Traces of these civil troubles may be found in the · Borough accounts, e.g. :—

		£	s.	d.
1645. For quartering Bristol soldiers going to Faringdon	... ...	1	16	0
1646. Paid to labourers, two days in throwing down the bulwarks	... ...	0	8	0
Paid Meades for carrying a letter to the Governor to remove the soldiers		0	1	6
1647, Feb. 24. Paid for quartering forty-eight horses and men of Col. Fleetwood's regiment	... ...	4	16	0
1648, Sept. 21. Paid for quartering eighteen horses one night with fire and candle		0	9	0

Judging from the accounts for the year 1649, the town had to pay far more for the support of the Commonwealth than it used in ordinary years to pay for the support of the

[e] Marshall, p. 197.   [f] Calendar State Papers, 1644-5, p. 280.
[g] Marshall, p. 203.

Monarchy; the total sum of £6 12s. 6d. was thus paid in five instalments during that year.

But the most noteworthy result of these disturbances in the municipal life of the town was that Mr. Edmund Hiorne, who had been Town Clerk since 1607, was deposed from that office; as Town Clerk he had signed the Chamberlains' accounts taken in December, 1642, but the next account, which was not taken till February, 1646, is signed by "Jo. Williams, Town Clerk." We have seen that Mr. Hiorne was reprimanded by the House of Commons for his zeal in the Royalist cause, and we may naturally assume that it was that zeal which led to his deposition. He appears to have shown his disgust at his treatment by withholding the rents that he owed to the town, as at the accounts taken in December, 1646, he is returned as owing arrears to the amount of £1 9s. 3d.

There are few persons now-a-days who have not read Sir Walter Scott's novel of "Woodstock," in which the skill of that great writer has so blended fiction and fact that it is hard to know where the one ends and the other begins. The substratum of fact is that when the Commissioners appointed by the Parliament to take possession of the royal property arrived at the Manor House they were frightened out of their senses by what they supposed to be supernatural visitations; their beds were raised and upset, trenchers were hurled at them, wood stacked in an adjoining room was violently thrown about; there were explosions and horrible noises; and all without any visible cause. For some time these occurrences were believed to be the work of the Evil One; but this belief was shattered when a clever royalist, Joe Collins by name, confessed that having obtained the post of clerk to the Commissioners he had contrived these things to impose on their credulity. But when Prince Charles was escaping after the battle of Worcester, his route did not lie through Woodstock, nor, according to the authorities, did Cromwell visit the town at that time.

Although Mr. Edmund Hiorne showed his loyalty by delivering the town armour to the Royalists, yet the old mace did not find its way to the Royal treasury, as many others did at that time; for in 1655[h] the Mayor, Mr. George Gregory, gave £3, and the Council voted £5 and the old mace for the purchase of a new mace, and as these amounts were insufficient an additional sum of £5 was voted by the Council at the next meeting. Some five years later, during the mayoralty of Thomas Glover, the mace was re-made, when probably the royal arms and initials and the crown were added.

During the period between the execution of Charles I and the restoration of Charles II the magistrates were allowed to perform the marriage ceremony. In the register preserved in the vestry of St. Mary's Church there are many entries of marriages so performed by the

THE MACE.

[h] Acts of Council, 24th October, 1655.

Justices of Woodstock, and it is noteworthy that these entries are in the handwriting of the minister for the time being, and not of any civil functionary. The following is the first of these entries :—

"1653. Mark Southam, of Enston in the County of Oxon, and Jane Barton, of Aynow in the same County (*sic*) were married upon the 24th day of December by Mr. Thomas Rayer, Justice of the Peace for this incorporation."

In such cases the banns were published in the market-place instead of in the church. There are entries of such publications of banns, of which the following is an example :

"1654. The marriage intended between Thomas Bishop, of Dean in the County of Oxon, and Marie Page, of Great Woolford in the County of Warwick, was published in the Market Place of Woodstock upon three several market days, *viz*. :—October the 17, October the 24, and October the 31."

After the Restoration all such marriages were confirmed by Act of Parliament.[i]

The most interesting record among the Acts of the Council for this time is that John Peterson was elected Beadle of the beggars, and scavenger. His duties were defined to be to "keep clean the gutter from the Crown door below the Guildhall, to look that no dogs come into the Church in service or sermon time, and to see that no children play in the Church or Churchyard on the Sabbath-day ; and to whip all offenders when he shall be commanded

[i] 12 Car. II, c. 32.

so to do"; and his salary was fixed at twenty shillings a year, and a coat, cap, and pair of shoes and stockings.[j] In 1689 this functionary's duties were further defined to include "keeping the beggars out of the town," and he was also provided with a wheelbarrow.

The Protector's Council during the interregnum appears to have been more solicitous for the spiritual welfare of the town than the King's Privy Council had been; for in 1656 it directed the Trustees for the maintenance of Ministers to settle an augmentation of £50 a year on the Minister at Woodstock.[k] When we remember how slight is the contribution made by New Woodstock to the stipend of the rector, we can see that this augmentation was a timely aid to the divine who then officiated at St. Mary's Church: at the same time it must be borne in mind that he was in all probability either a Presbyterian or an Independent.

After the Restoration the Borough was visited by a Royal Commission under an Act of Parliament "for the well governing and regulating of Corporations." The Commission, which was composed of Oxfordshire gentlemen of position,[l] on the 10th July, 1662, "deemed it expedient for the public safety to displace, remove, and discharge . . . . . Mr. Alexander Johnson the present Mayor of the Borough of New Woodstock, Mr. Miles Fleetwood, a Common Councillor, Mr. Williams, Town Clerk," and three other

[j] Acts of Council, 28th April, 1654.

[k] Calendar State Papers, 1655-6, p. 211.

[l] They were Sir Anthony Cope of Hanwell, Sir Thomas Spencer of Yarnton, Sir Francis Henry Lee of Ditchley, Sir Thomas Peniston of Cornwell, Compton Reade, Esq., Sir William Knollys of Thame, William Cope, Esq., Sir Rowland Lacy of Shipton-under-Wychwood, Sir Littleton Osbaldeston of Chadlington, and Thomas Wheate, Esq., of Glympton (High Sheriff of Oxfordshire in 1665).

Councillors "from any further exercise of their said places"; and appointed Alderman Thomas Glover to be Mayor. At the same time the Commissioners restored Mr. Edmund Hiorne to the Town Clerkship, from which he had been deposed during the Civil War; but he did not long survive to enjoy his restored dignity, for he died in 1663, and was succeeded as Town Clerk by George Ryves. The original order of the Commissioners is pasted into the Book of Acts of the Council of this date, and their seals attached to the order are in as good preservation as when they were originally affixed.

It was not long after his Restoration that Charles II granted a new Charter[m] to the Borough, which as we have already noticed did little more than give the sanction of the Crown to the Constitution adopted by the Council in 1580; but there is one noteworthy omission : no mention is made of the freemen or their privileges. This omission did not mean that the class of freemen had ceased to exist ; for the Acts of the Council show that till 1886 the Council continued to elect freemen ; and, as we have before noticed, in 1728 (some sixty years after this Charter) a man was fined for trading within the Borough, he not being free of the same. By this Charter the Crown obtained further powers over the Corporation by the provisions which, while continuing to the Council the election of any new High Steward, Recorder, or Town Clerk, required the sanction of the Crown before the appointment was complete. The Mayor, High Steward, Recorder, and Aldermen were appointed *ex officio* Magistrates of the Borough, but as their

[m] Dated 24th August, 1665.

names had hitherto been included in the Commissions of the Peace this provision did not make much practical difference. The election of the Mayor was reserved to the Mayor and Commonalty, and the election of a Common Councillor to the surviving members of the Council. One new power was conferred on the Mayor, by which he was authorized to search houses for hidden corn on market days, and carry any that might be found into the market and there sell it at a reasonable price.

The records of the Acts of the Council, which are fragmentary from 1650 to 1665, are very full indeed after 1669, and show that the Council interfered or attempted to interfere in almost every department of the life of the town. Every inhabitant of the Borough was ordered "to shovel up the dirt before his door in the street, and carry the dirt away within the space of one week," under the penalty of three shillings and fourpence." In 1693 payments were directed to be made "to the undertakers to bring water to to the Town "; but this undertaking does not seem to have been carried out. Apart from the erection of a Town Hall, the cost of which was defrayed by Lord Lovelace, and of a Market House," the only public work of importance that appears to have been executed during the latter half of the seventeenth century was that ordered on 19th May, 1696, when "it was agreed that the wooden bridge be new made, and that it be made with stone." With regard to the Town Hall, it was agreed that Mr. Cary "have a lease of

---

ᵃ Acts of Council, 14th March, 1662.

ᵒ Probably the Market House shown in the illustration facing page 61. It would seem to have consisted merely of a roof, in the centre of which stood the Market Cross.

the Town Hall for twenty-one years, excepting out of his lease the Council Chamber, the Engine House and a way thereto, and the prison."[p] The engine referred to was possibly a fire-engine presented to the town by Lord Norreys in 1681, when the Council visited him to return thanks, and one pound was voted from the Borough Fund to be given to his servants.

Other resolutions relate to the Market and the Grammar School. In 1669 and again in 1672 leases of the tolls of the Market were granted to private individuals at the rent of £10 a year. Regulations were made concerning the length and disposition of stalls and the rates charged for them; for instance, the Council ordered that "no huckster or haggler or any other person who buys to sell again in kind .... shall be permitted to buy any butter, cheese, fish, fowl, or eggs within this Borough before the ringing of the market bell .... upon the penalty of three shillings and fourpence."[q] And later, they ordered "that the sergeant and constables do throw down Joseph Fletcher's stall where it usually stands on Market days, because it stands out of the Market and is a common nuisance."[r] The worthy Councillors evidently thought that too many holidays spoilt the school-boys, for they ordered[s] "that if any person shall come to our free school to ellect (*sic*) a Play Day it shall not be granted unless he pay for the same two shillings and sixpence, but if he be above the degree of an Esquire, five shillings, and that the money be employed in buying books." Then follows an order "that no wine be given to any person till the town shall be out of debt."

[p] Acts of Council, 6th December, 1684. [q] Ib., July, 1670.
[r] Ib., 27th July, 1685. [s] Ib., 24th September, 1677.

Moreover, the Council did not confine its attention to the civil affairs of the town, but exercised control over the Church. They appointed the Parish Clerk with the consent of Mr. Widdows, Curate to Dr. Goode;[t] they directed that " the Churchwardens do make an agreement and cause to be new plastered and ceiled that part of the chancel which lies unceiled ";[u] they granted Mr. Cary "a little seat wherein now sit Peter Franklyn, John Bruce, and Robert Hatley for his maids to sit in ;"[v] they ordered the pulpit be moved to the other side of the Church ;[w] and that " the Churchwardens do move the young men that sit in the seats above the pulpit and place them in such places as they think fit."[x] At this time the Council seems in fact to have exercised all the powers of the vestry, and it is noteworthy that at least on one occasion the Mayor signs the minutes of the Vestry meeting before the Rector.[y]

The Churchwardens' accounts for this period show that the good people of Woodstock were not wanting in liberality, as can easily be proved by a few extracts showing the amounts collected on briefs :—

	£	s.	d.
1686, May 16. Collected for the persecuted French Protestants	32	6	4
1689, July. Collected for the Irish Protestants	6	0	0
1691. June 24. Collected for the relief of the inhabitants of Teignmouth and Sheldon in the County of Devon (whereof one groat not current) ...	0	19	5

[t] Acts of Council, 27th March, 1675.   [u] Ib., 8th April, 1678.
     [v] Ib., 8th May, 1679.   [w] Ib., 29th January, 1683.
[x] Ib., 6th June, 1683.   [y] Churchwardens' Accounts, 21st April, 1663.

1693, Oct. 29.   Collected for the Redemption
        of Captives in Algiers, Sally, &c.   4 13   5

On several occasions the Minister and Churchwardens granted certificates that certain persons had not been touched for the King's Evil;[1] and on one occasion it is recorded that " George Hawthorn having been excom-

THE RECTORY.

municated was this day according to the Decree of Court absolved from his excommunication."[2]

We have already noticed that the Borough was part of the Parish of Bladon, and that its inhabitants were dependent on the Rector of Bladon for spiritual ministrations, which during the early part of the century at all events were

[1] Ib., 16th March, 1686, *et seq.*   [2] Ib., 20th July, 1684.

very scanty. That the inhabitants might not be obliged to go to Bladon when they wished to see their spiritual adviser, and that he might be at hand for baptisms, marriages, funerals, and the like services, Bishop Fell in 1686 bought the lease of a house let by the Corporation to Peter Franklin for eighty years, and built a good house that the Rector of Bladon might ever afterwards " for the good of the inhabitants of the Borough reside amongst them." He surrendered the lease to the Mayor and Commonalty, who declared that they held the property in trust to permit the Rector of Bladon to inhabit the house, and if he did not do so, to let it to a tenant and apply the rents for the relief of the poor. The house was thus let in 1809, and £14 paid to the Mayor for the poor, which he devoted to a local fund.

An interesting experiment was begun in the year 1677, when the Council agreed that trial be made for one year to set the poor of this town to work upon the employment of " silk-winding, and that trial after be made for one year to employ the said poor upon the trade of clothing and blanketing, and which of them shall prove most convenient and advantageous to be continued."[b] But we are told nothing of the success or failure of these experiments.

Fuller records of the usefulness of the View of Frankpledge have come to us from this period than from the period before the Civil War. The jury continued to present those who committed nuisances injurious to the public health ; thus Sir Littleton Osbaldeston, of Chadlington, who was tenant of one of the Corporation meadows, and M.P. for

[b] Acts of Council, 2nd Feb., 1676-7.

the Borough in 1678, was twice at least presented for not cleaning the Back Brook belonging to his meadow.° On the latter of these two occasions the jury presented three men for their muck-hills before their doors, and three men and a woman for not coming to church the last Sunday, for which they were fined one shilling each. An indictment was ordered to be brought in against Mr. Metcalf for holding a conventicle in his house; and Widow Dissell was presented for entertaining her daughter for the space of a month contrary to the statute, and the daughter is ordered to " be removed to her husband on Monday next if she depart not herself before." This order was made that she might not obtain a settlement in the town, and so become chargeable to the poor rates, her proper settlement being at her husband's home.

More noteworthy than all the other records in the Books of the Acts of the Council are those which show the keen interest taken by the Council in contemporary politics. The interference of Parliament in 1662 when the then Mayor was deposed for his anti-Royalist tendencies, had evidently been a lesson to the members of the Corporation, for from the year 1677 onwards we find that they were Tories of the most pronounced type. Their unquestioning faith in all the revelations relating to the supposed Popish plot which revived the fears of the Inquisition of Spain in the minds of all good Protestants, led them to confer on " Titus Oates, Doctor of Divinity," the freedom of the Boroughᵈ : but there is no record of their having disfranchised him when all his perjuries

---

° Book of Acts of Portmouth Court, 21st April, 1667, and 8th Oct., 1673.

were found out. When Charles II issued a Proclamation, which purported to annul without the consent of Parliament the penal laws against the Dissenters, the Council agreed " *nemine contradicente* that an address be made to His Majesty to give him thanks for his gracious Declaration which was lately read in our Church."[e] After the discovery of the Rye House Plot the Council agreed that " an address be made to His Majesty shewing their detestation of that horrid treason contrived against his person, his Royal brother, and these kingdoms, and to congratulate His Majesty for his safe deliverance from the said treason."[f]

When James II ascended the throne, the Mayor, Aldermen and Town Clerk went " to London with an address to congratulate His Majesty," and their expenses were defrayed out of the Borough Fund[g]; and some years later when he visited the Manor House, he was presented with twenty broad pieces of gold in a white satin purse[h]: nay, further, they actually surrendered their liberties to the King; for they " unanimously agreed upon the serving Mr. Mayor with a writ of *quo warranto* that a full submission be made unto His Majesty's writ[i]"; and two days later they sealed a document by which the Charter was surrendered to the King. As, however, he did not wish to disfranchise the Borough, but merely to remodel their constitution, he granted a new Charter (dated 27th August, 1688) in which the only important change seems to have been that the members of the Council were excused from taking

d Acts of Council, 17th Sept., 1679.   e Ib., 31st May, 1681.

f Ib., 24th July, 1683.   g Ib., 23rd Feb., 1684-5.

h Ib., 29th August, 1687.   i Ib., 18th January, 1687-8.

the oaths of allegiance and supremacy, from partaking
of the Lord's Supper according to the rites of the Church
of England, and from making the Declaration against
Popish Recusants. The practical effect of this clause was
that membership of the Council, which had hitherto been
restricted to communicants of the Church of England, was
now thrown open to Protestant Dissenters and to Roman
Catholics.

But already the King might have seen the hand-writing
upon the wall; not two months had elapsed after the new
Council had been sworn in, before William of Orange
landed at Torbay; six weeks later, William was in St.
James's Palace, and James an exile flying for France.
Before, however, the latter had thrown the Great Seal into
the Thames, he issued from Faversham a last proclamation
reinstating all Charters the surrender of which had not been
enrolled, and annulling the Charters which he had granted
upon these surrenders.[j] And so the Charter of James
was not in force for more than four months.

The Corporation of Woodstock received the accession of
William and Mary in sullen silence; and it was not till the
death of Queen Mary had plunged the whole nation into
mourning that they had any dealings with King William;
then they presented him with an address of condolence.[k]
They had previously provided a barrel of ale and five dozen
of bread and cakes on the Thanksgiving Day in November,
1692, after the naval victory of La Hogue.[l] Queen Anne's
accession was welcomed with great jubilation, a hogshead

---

[j] Merewether and Stephen, History of Boroughs, pp. 1836-8.
[k] Acts of Council, 1st Feb., 1694-5. [l] Ib., 7th Nov., 1602.

of ale, twenty dozen of cakes, five dozen Wiggs (*sic*), a dozen of claret and a dozen of sack, were provided for the Day of the Proclamation, the wine probably for the members of the Council ;[m] and eight days later "an address was sealed to be presented to Her Majesty condoling the death of the King, and congratulating Her Majesty's accession to the Throne."[n]

[m] Acts of Council, 16th March, 1701-2.   [n] Ib., 24th March, 1701-2.

BLENHEIM PALACE, NORTH FRONT.

CHAPTER VII.

The Building of Blenheim.

WITH the reign of Queen Anne a new period begins in the history of Woodstock. Hitherto Woodstock Park had belonged to the Kings of England, and the Manor House had been only occasionally visited by them, so that the inhabitants of Woodstock could not be greatly affected by any influence which the occupants of the House might wish to exert. Now, however, the Park and Manor House were handed over to the most powerful subject of the day, who was provided at the Queen's expense with a lordly mansion, and changed the very name of the place, so that generations to come might remember his prowess and forget that Blenheim Park had ever known royal owners. Not content with changing the name, his descendants formed the lake and the gardens, and so changed the aspect of the country that Fair Rosamund would lose her way should she ever be allowed to revisit those bowers where once she dallied with her Royal lover.

To recount the history of the first Duke of Marlborough would be to recapitulate the history of England during his life. "Handsome Jack Churchill," as he was called in his younger days, was the son of a poor cavalier from Wiltshire, and began his career as an ensign in the foot-guards. He gained his first experiences of warfare in 1673, when he was sent with his regiment to help the French in the Netherlands, where he won the respect of all with whom he came in contact. After his return from this war he was rewarded with a Scotch peerage and the command of the only regiment of dragoons ; and in the first year of the reign of James II he was appointed an Ambassador Extraordinary to the Court of Louis XIV. Later he was employed as second in command against the Duke of Monmouth, and after the victory of Sedgemoor, which was entirely due to his genius, and the Bloody Assizes (when on a single circuit Jeffries hanged 320 men and women for alleged complicity in Monmouth's rebellion), proved himself a true man by interceding with the King for the condemned prisoners. Although he owed his fortune and position to James, yet he would never desert his Protestant principles, and when William of Orange was nearing London on his triumphal march from Devonshire, he left his old master and threw in his lot with the Protestant party. But William's cool treatment of his new adherent was distasteful to his pride, and he thereupon began to intrigue with the exiled king,[a] until the death of Queen Mary without issue made it certain that if the Princess Anne, with whom his wife was on more than ordinary terms of friendship, survived King William, she would at his death ascend the throne.

Her reign was the zenith of Churchill's glory. Immediately after Anne become Queen he was appointed Captain-General of the forces at home and abroad, and at once took the field in the Netherlands against all the power of Louis XIV. Victory after victory crowned his arms, until on 13th August, 1704, at the little village of Blenheim, he inflicted a crushing defeat on the French and thus saved the Empire. He had been created Duke of Marlborough at the end of the campaign of 1702 ; but after Blenheim, the first important victory of the British arms on the continent since Agincourt, the gratitude of the nation knew no bounds. The honour and manor of Woodstock with its members, comprising seven smaller manors or reputed manors, the ruined Manor House, Woodstock Park (1793 acres in extent), and some five hundred and thirty-six acres of land without the Park were granted to him and his heirs for ever ; the only acknowledgment which was reserved to the Crown being that on the anniversary of the battle, every future owner of the property should present to the King or Queen a small flag emblazoned with three fleur-de-lys. But these magnificent gifts did not exhaust the Queen's gratitude. She gave him out of her Civil List

---

[a] In so doing he was only following the example of most of the leading statesmen of his day, even of the Cabinet Ministers ; and, as was said by the Duke of Wellington, "it was no more than many men did in France during Napoleon's reign." Wolseley's Marlborough, ii., 232.

sums amounting to no less than £240,000 for the erection of a house which should worthily hand down to posterity the memory of her hero's deeds and her own gratitude.

Sir John Vanbrugh was employed as architect, and on a site on the south side of the valley, opposite the ruins of the Manor House, erected a mansion which is without its equal in the British Isles. The general design of the building is classic, but it is the pseudo-classicism of the Italian Renaissance rather than the severer style of ancient Greece and Rome. The south front, which is surmounted by a bust of Louis XIV, taken from the gate of Tournay, gives the impression of dignity, affluence, and comfort; while on the north side the architect has given full play to his imagination, and has contrived to erect a façade which will for ever live in the memory of every one who beholds it. True, Pope's spiteful epigram on Vanbrugh involuntarily comes to the mind of most who see the Palace for the first time :—

> "Lie heavy on him, Earth, for he
> Laid many a heavy load on thee;"

but gradually the imposing dignity of the work, the massive structure of the buildings, and the completeness of the whole design give one an exalted idea of the genius of the architect. But Vanbrugh's powers of calculation were not equal to his abilities as a designer, and the consequence was that the cost was under-estimated and the work frequently stopped for want of money; finally "in 1721 the disputes culminated in a lawsuit successfully brought against the Duke by the workmen for arrears of pay, the defendants' contention being that the Treasury was liable for the cost."[b]

[b] Duke of Marlborough, in *Pall Mall Magazine*, August, 1894.

SOUTH FRONT OF BLENHEIM PALACE.

And in the next year, when Vanbrugh and his wife came to visit Blenheim, they were by the order of the Duchess prevented from entering the Palace, and so were obliged to stay at an inn in Woodstock.[c]

One suggestion of Vanbrugh's was overruled by the Duchess of Marlborough, to the lasting regret of all antiquarians : he proposed that the ruins of the old Manor House should be left as they were ; but the Duchess apparently thought that this suggestion covered a deep design on his part to secure "an agreeable lodging" for himself ; and ordered the ruins to be pulled down and the materials used in the new building. But

ENTRANCE GATEWAY.

on the other hand he overruled her protests and erected thirty-three rooms (as a cool retreat in summer) in the bridge joining the northern and southern sides of the valley, and leading straight from the north entrance of the Palace to the lofty pillar erected on the Plain. At this time the

[c] D'Israeli : Curiosities of Literature, v, 191, et seq., containing an account of the squabbles between Vanbrugh and the Duke and Duchess.

enormous arch spanned a little rivulet scarcely ten feet broad, and thereby justified a second epigram of Pope's :—

> " The minnows, as through this vast arch they pass,
>   Cry, How like whales we look, thanks to your Grace !"[d]

However, when a few years later " Capability " Brown laid out the gardens, he dammed the stream at the southern end of the valley to form the lake, and thus, to quote Dr. Johnson, "drowned the epigram."

Those who are not admirers of classic architecture will perhaps prefer to visit the High Lodge, which lies in the older part of the Park between Combe and Bladon; it consists of a central tower of three storeys in height, with square wings one storey lower on the right and left; the walls are surmounted with battlements, and the whole gives the impression of strength and age; apparently it dates from the sixteenth century. The view from the High Lodge is magnificent; situated on the high land to the north-west of the Evenlode valley, it looks right across that valley and over Handborough and Eynsham to the Wytham woods and to the Berkshire downs as far as Faringdon clump; while on the north and west it is shut in by the forest, the old oaks of which may possibly have been standing when the Plantagenets lived at the Manor House. Here died the notorious Earl of Rochester, who had been appointed Ranger of the Park by Charles II. In all the profligate orgies of that profligate court, Rochester led the way; during the whole of five years, it is said, he was never sober;

---

[d] This is quoted and attributed to Pope in the Duke of Marlborough's article above referred to ; but I have been able to find neither it nor the epigram previously quoted in any edition of Pope's works.

THE HIGH LODGE, BLENHEIM.

and, a prematurely old man, he retreated to this secluded spot to spend his last days. During his last illness he was visited by Bishop Burnet, who convinced him of the error of his ways and urged him to make his peace with God.

Since its establishment at Blenheim the family of Marlborough has been very closely connected with the town of Woodstock, and many notes of this connection appear in the Borough Records. Almost immediately after the estate was granted to the first Duke he was made a freeman of the Borough, a member of the Council, and High Steward of the Borough ; and every succeeding Duke in turn held that high office so long as the Old Corporation was in existence. The first Duke apparently showed his appreciation of the honour by paving a portion of the town[e] ; his widow on one occasion at least clothed forty poor men and forty poor women of the town at her own expense, for which the Council thanked her[f] ; in 1776 the second Duke built and presented to the town the Town Hall, which is now standing in the Market Place. And later Dukes have earned the gratitude of the townsfolk by supplying them with pure water from the water works at Blenheim.

[e] Acts of Council, 3rd March, 1718.
Ib., 29th Sept., 1731.

OLD STAIRCASE IN POST OFFICE.

CHAPTER VIII.

—

Municipal Decay.

THE building of Blenheim begins an epoch in the history of the Borough of Woodstock which closes with the accession of Queen Victoria, and is for the most part by no means exciting. The Council seems to have exerted its influence in the same manner as it acted during the latter part of the previous century; the only difference appears to have been that the members of the Council were too much inclined to use the Borough property for their own advantage rather than for the advantage of the inhabitants at large. This feature appears in the first decade of the century, when one of the Corporation meadows was divided between two tenants who, in addition to the rent to be paid to the Chamberlains for the use of the town, were obliged to provide, the one a couple of pullets, and the other a leg of pork, for the Mayor's Banquet.[a] This system was followed till the end of the century, when a large repast was supplied by the tenants of the various properties. The leases that were in force in 1800 reserved to the Mayor two neats' tongues and an adder from the tenant of Pyed Bull (now the Grammar School), two couple of rabbits from the tenant of the adjoining house, a leg of mutton weighing eight pounds from the tenant of the New Angel,[b] a rump of beef weighing twenty pounds from the tenant of the house now the Post Office, a leg of pork from the tenant of the King's Arms, and a couple of fat pullets from the tenant of a house which now forms part of the Woodstock Arms. Moreover, when in 1715 the Council leased certain property in the Back Lane to William Diston for him to build a cockpit, they stipulated that "the Common Councilmen of the said Borough shall have the liberty of going into the pit at any cock-matches to be fought there without paying anything for the same,"[c] but they were not to sit in the seat nearest the pit. Some twenty years later the Council took Sir William Thomson's water for three years at twenty shillings a year, when it was "agreed that it shall not be fished by any one Common Councilman singly nor by less than two being present, and that nobody shall be licensed to fish but by the majority of the Corpora-

[a] Acts of Council, 21st July, 1703.
[b] Now occupied by Mr. George Scarsbrook.
[c] Acts of Council, 20th July, 1715.

tion."[d] Owing to the restricted area of the Borough there has never been any difficulty in securing tenants for the meadows ; but in 1759 the members of the Council resolved that instead of letting them to the highest bidder, they themselves would draw lots for them, and that if the draw should assign a meadow to any Councilman who did not want to occupy it, he should not let it to any outsider if another Councilman wished to take it.[e]

The Mayor's salary, which was twelve guineas in 1738,[f] was raised to sixteen guineas in 1756, £25 in 1797, and to £40 in 1807 ; while beer and wine flowed freely whenever there was the slightest excuse. The Council agreed that the same money should be expended at the proclamation of King George II as was expended at the proclamation of Queen Anne[g]; at the Proclamation of Peace in 1749 they gave half a hogshead of ale and thirty dozen cakes to the populace, and spent £1 11s. 6d. on music, and £2 5s. at the Bear on themselves.[h] Three years later the following item is entered in the Chamberlains' account book :—

> 1752, April 16. Paid to Mr. Cross at the
> Bear for the Mayor and gentlemen
> regaling themselves after a trouble-
> some day's business   ...   ... £1 3s. 0d.

When the first stone of the new Town Hall was laid the workmen were treated to half a hogshead of ale[i]; and

---

[d] Acts of Council, 10th January, 1735-6.   [e] Ib., 14th Sept., 1759.

[f] The Chamberlains' accounts are missing before 1738, but are perfect from that date to the present time.

[g] Acts of Council, 19th June, 1727. See p. 102.

[h] Ib., 4th March, 1748-9.   [i] Ib., 21st March, 1766.

when the roof was erected they had double that quantity.[j] Twelve months later the Corporation audited the Chamberlains' accounts in the new Town Hall, and dined in the Council Chamber for the first time at a cost of £3 19s. 5½d.[k] And in 1802 Mr. Francis Burton alleged as his reason for resigning the Recordership that "my loss of sight deprives me of the power of joining without inconvenience in the festivities which accompany our annual meeting," i.e., the Petty Sessions and View of Frankpledge.[l]

Not content with spending the town funds on themselves, the Council began to gamble with them. In 1747 a lottery ticket was bought, and it was agreed that if it came up a prize it should be applied towards building a new Town Hall[m]; two more tickets were bought in the following year, a fourth in 1751, and a fifth in 1755; but the Council never won a prize.

The Council had evidently been led to speculate by the success of Sir Robert Cocks the Rector, who in 1719 "purchased several tickets in the then lottery, and before the drawing thereof publicly declared that if any of them should come up a prize he would apply the money to the use of the poor of New Woodstock.[n]" He gained a prize of £1000, which he sold for £800, and during his life he applied the interest for the use of the town; after his death the principal was employed to purchase a farm at Arncott (now about seventy-nine acres) the rents of which were to be applied for

[j] Ib., 18th November, 1766.

[k] Chamberlains' Accounts, 10th December, 1767.

[l] Acts of Council, 23rd July, 1802.   [m] Ib., 2nd November, 1747.

[n] Charity Reports, 1819-35, Oxon. 491.

clothing eight poor children, for apprenticing one of the
children, and for schooling. The income of this endowment
is now applied to the National School.

The Council continued to show their interest in contemporary politics during the period now under discussion. We
have noticed the rejoicings in the town at the proclamation
of George II, and of the Peace of Aix la Chapelle ; another
hogshead of ale was given to the populace on the Thanksgiving Day for the suppression of the Rebellion of 1745.[o]
In the discussions on the Regency Bill in 1789 the Council
supported Pitt, and at a special meeting voted their thanks
to him, to their "two worthy representatives, and to the
other 265 patriotic members of the House of Commons, for
their strenuous support of the Constitutional Right of the
Lords and Commons of this Realm to provide the means of
supplying the defect of the personal exercise of the Royal
Authority arising from the indisposition of His Majesty"[p] ;
and three months later they voted an address to the King
congratulating him on his recovery.[q] In the next year they
desired their members " to oppose the repealing of the Test
and Corporation Acts, which experience has shown are the
best security of our Civil and Religious Liberties."[r]

Before the war with the French Republic the Corporation
paid £3 12s. "for a hogshead of ale given to the populace
on burning the effigy of Thomas Pain," presumably the
well-known free-thinker and advocate of the Rights of
Man.[s] The ringers were paid a guinea for ringing on

[o] Acts of Council, 7th October, 1746.   [p] Ib., 12th January, 1789.
[q] Ib., 28th March, 1789.   [r] Ib., 15th February, 1790.
[s] Chamberlains' Accounts, 4th January, 1793.

account of Admiral Nelson's victory over the French at the Battle of the Nile,[t] and another at the fall of Seringapatam[u]; but no notice was taken either of Trafalgar or Waterloo: the worthy Councillors evidently thought that the marriage of Princess Charlotte of Wales and Prince Leopold of Saxe Coburg was of more importance than the latter battle, and more worthy the presentation of an address to the Prince Regent.[v] In 1807, after the Catholic Emancipation Bill had been withdrawn and Granville's ministry had resigned rather than pledge itself never again to touch the question, the Council voted an address to the King thanking him for the signal testimony of his unalterable attachment and conscientious regard to the Protestant Establishment,[w] and in 1821[x] and 1822[y] they sent two petitions to the House of Lords against Catholic Emancipation.

In 1798 and again in 1803 there were two noteworthy outbursts of patriotism. In February, 1798, the Council agreed that the Mayor's salary should be reduced from £25 to £5 a year, that no entertainment should be given by the Council for five years, and that during that time £50 a year should be subscribed towards the expenses of the Government[z]; but the first part of that resolution was rescinded in the following August,[a] and no subscription was ever made towards the expenses of Government. In the month of April in that same year, after reading a letter from the Secretary of State, the Council resolved to hold a meeting of the inhabitants in the Town Hall to consider

---

[t] Ib., 9th October, 1798.   [u] Ib., 15th September, 1799.
[v] Acts of Council, 13th June, 1816.   [w] Ib., 27th April, 1807.
[x] Ib., 21st April, 1821.   [y] Ib., 28th May, 1822.   [z] Ib., 24th Feb, 1798.

the formation "of an Armed Association to assist the Civil Power as occasion may require in the preservation of peace, and to suppress every tendency to tumult and disorder within this Borough.[b]" But the Borough Records give no further information about this meeting or its results.

The second occasion was at the beginning of the war with Napoleon in 1803, when a large number of the inhabitants of the Borough presented to the Corporation a paper "offering to associate themselves as Volunteers to be trained and exercised for the defence of the Realm in the present emergency." The Council "resolved that too great commendation cannot be bestowed on the inhabitants of this place for the spirit, zeal, and distinguished loyalty with which they have come forward upon the present occasion in defence of their King and Country. That the same ought as far as possible to be encouraged, and that no time should be lost in making proper arrangements for forming such Volunteers into a Military body to be called the Loyal Woodstock Volunteers." A subscription was to be started to defray their expenses. Lord Francis Spencer was suggested as Commander, and Mr. Blackstone the Recorder as a subordinate officer.[c] The Council's share in the subscription consisted not of a money contribution, but of beer, which was supplied to the Volunteers at a cost of £11 1s. 8d., a sum which at the prices of the time paid for about three hogsheads.

It will be remembered that till the Reform Bill of 1832 the freemen of the Borough returned two members to Parliament. There is among the Borough documents a

* Ib., 27th Aug, 1798. [b] Ib., 28th April, 1798. [c] Ib., 11th April, 1803.

"Bill of Expenses upon Mr. Bertie's and Sir John Walters' account in 1705." This obviously refers to the contested election in that year, when the Honourable Charles Bertie and Mr. William Cadogan were elected. The total amounts to £105 3s., and its nature can easily be guessed from the first few items :—

MR. GLOVER'S BILL.	£	s.	d.
Feb. 15, 1704-5. For a hogshead of ale ...	3	0	0
For fire, bread, cheese, and pipes	0	15	0
April 19 (1705). For a hogshead of ale ...	3	0	0
For fire, cheese, and butter ...	0	8	0
For ale and victuals at several times for out-town Freemen ...	2	10	0
May 11. For victuals upon the day of election for forty Freemen	2	0	0
For a hogshead of ale then ...	3	0	0
For hay and corn for the Earl of Abingdon's[d] horses	0	1	0
	£15	3	0

About £22 was "put into Mr. Bushton's hands on his journey to London to solicit and take care of the London Freemen."

A rough draft of a letter in the Town Clerk's writing to Mr. Bertie, dated 25th June, 1706, appears to be connected with this election. The usual fee to the Town Clerk for preparing the indentures signifying the result was two guineas ; there was also paid " to the Sergeant half-a-guinea,

---

[d] He was either the brother or uncle of Mr. Bertie.

the Cryer who cleans the hall five shillings, to the Ringers a guinea, and those that carried you in the chair a guinea."

A few years later there was an election petition, in which the petitioners alleged that the other candidates had prevailed with the Mayor to make new freemen for the purpose of the election ; and insisted that the right of election lay with the Mayor, Aldermen, Councillors, and Freemen residing as well without as within the Borough ; while the sitting Member insisted that the right was only in the resident Freemen. The Committee of the House of Commons (to whom the petition was referred) resolved that the right was in the Mayor, Aldermen, and Freemen,[e] thus (say Merewether and Stephens[f]) "apparently negativing the right of the non-residents."

In 1722 another petition was presented, in which the petitioners alleged that at the election the Mayor, Brotherton, made a number of freemen who had no right to their freedom. This petition seems to have been dropped, as there is no recorded decision upon it.[g] It is, however, interesting to note that the honorary freedom of the Borough was conferred on no less than fifty-three gentlemen of the neighbourhood on the 12th January, 1722. John Skynner, who was elected M.P. in 1771, gave the town £80 for the erection of a Workhouse,[h] and in 1842 "Mr. Taylor paid into the hands of the Coal Committee a sum of £20 as a donation from F. Thesiger, Esq. (afterwards Lord Chelms-

---

[e] Journals H.C. xvii., 479 and 498.   [f] History of Boroughs, 1304.
[g] Journals H.C., xx, 21.   [h] Acts of Council, 16th August, 1771.

THE MARKET PLACE, WOODSTOCK, 1777.

ford and M.P., 1840-4), and a promise of five guineas per annum as long as he was Member for the Borough."[i]

·The works done by the Corporation during the eighteenth century consisted chiefly of repairs to the Causeway and Holloway; part of the town was pitched with pebbles;[j] one of the houses belonging to the Corporation was made into an Infirmary;[k] the Almshouse was rebuilt;[l] as people declined sending their children to school in cold weather on account of there being no fire, a chimney was erected in the Schoolroom;[m] the wells in Sheep Street and at the Town's End were mended and secured with good lids;[n] the old Town Hall was pulled down, "it being the judgment of skilful workmen that it was dangerous to assemble therein,"[o] and a new one was built at the expense of the Duke of Marlborough; a new well was dug in the Common Acre,[p] the old Market Cross and Market House were pulled down, and a new Market House or Shambles erected,[q] the builder being allowed the wood of the Market Cross and Pennyless Bench; and a Workhouse was built.[r] The Stocks and Pillory were erected on the hill in the Horse Fair;[s] and the Cage was put into repair.[t]

A few rules were made on matters which are now considered to belong to the department of Public Health; any one firing "his chimney so that it flames out above the top of his chimney" was to be fined 6s. 8d.[u]; the inhabitants

---

[i] Ib., 25th Feb,, 1842. [j] Ib., 16th April, 1716; 26th March, 1717.
[k] Ib., 23rd Oct., 1719. [l] Ib., 23rd March, 1724.
[m] Ib., 15th Oct., 1744. [n] Ib., 7th May, 1753. [o] Ib., 12th May, 1757.
[p] C.A., 4th Feb., 1766. [q] Ib., 2nd May, 1766. [r] Ib., 12th May, 1777.
[s] Ib., 3rd May, 1768. [t] Ib., 2nd May, 1763. [u] Ib., 29th Dec., 1709.

were ordered "to sweep and make clean the ground against
their respective houses so far as it is pitched with pebbles,"
and the Chamberlains were ordered to cart away the dirt
every Saturday morning[v]; a scavenger was appointed to
clean the two streets leading to the Park Gate[w]; and it was
agreed that the inhabitants of the Parish of Tackley should
be "indicted at the next Sessions if the road leading from
the Turnpike Road near Weevely to the Banbury Turnpike
Road were not well repaired before that time."[x]   In 1768
the Duke of Marlborough presented twelve lamps to the
town, which the Council agreed to light at the expense of
the Corporation[y]; who in 1772 paid £2 13s. for lighting
the lamps, and £11 6s. for oil, &c., from 1st October to
3rd April; later the lamps were lighted by public subscription, to which the Council gave £4 4s.

The freemen continued to pay fees on their admission in
lieu of buckets; during the greater part of this time the fee
was 5s.   But these buckets were not sufficient for the pro-
tection of the town against fire : a new engine was bought
in 1747 at a cost of £42, towards which the Corporation
contributed £19 6s., and the balance was raised by subscription[z]; and the fire-engines were ordered to be oiled
and repaired and played about the streets twice in every
year at the expense of the Corporation.[a]   Four years later
the vestry agreed with Mr. Chapman to lay six or more fire
plugs in the streets, and to keep them, and also the two fire

[v] Ib., 2nd Nov., 1713.   [w] Ib., 24th March, 1714-5.
[x] Ib., 27th Nov., 1759,   [y] Ib., 27th Dec. 1768.
[z] Chamberlains' Accounts, 21st January, 1747.
[a] Acts of Council, 24th August, 1773.

engines, pipes, and buckets in good repair.[b] Mr. Brown was to receive two guineas yearly for looking after the engines[c]; in 1807 a sum of £5 was voted to the Mayor to be distributed to those most deserving who assisted at the fire at Mrs. Bellenger's.[d] In 1790 Mr. Benjamin Bennett presented from the Phœnix Fire Office twelve leather buckets for the use of the Corporation[e]; and in 1829 the County Fire Office at the request of the Corporation gave a new fire-engine on condition that a proper place was provided for it.[f]

In connection with the Market the chief work of the eighteenth century was the building of the new Shambles to which reference has already been made: this building was not pulled down till 1870; all the butchers in the town, whether freemen or not, were obliged to take stalls and sell their meat there.[g] In 1735 notice was given that if any maltster or corn-dealer sold corn by sample within the Borough, both the seller and the buyer should be prosecuted as the law directed[h]; and a fortnight later a reward of ten shillings was offered to every one who would give information of disobedience to this notice. In 1731 the tolls of cattle (except horses) were let at £8 a year[i]; and the other tolls at £20[j]; but they appear to have decreased in value as they were afterwards let at prices decreasing from £22 10s. in 1772[k] to £6 in 1802.[l]

[b] Churchwardens' Accounts, 31st August, 1777.
[c] Acts of Council, 24th Dec., 1792.   [d] Ib., 7th Dec., 1807.
[e] Ib., 24th December, 1790.   [f] Ib., 6th July, 1829.
[g] Ib., 4th Oct., 1766.   [h] Ib., 21st Jan., 1734-5.
[i] Ib., 2nd Dec., 1731.   [j] Ib., 4th April, 1732.
[k] Ib., 4th Feb., 1772.   [l] Ib., 2nd Dec., 1802.

At the beginning of the eighteenth century the Council still continued to exercise some control over the Church; a new gallery was ordered to be erected in 1713 under the arch leading to the belfry for the accommodation of the Churchwardens, Constables, and Overseers;[m] but the jurisdiction of the Council was quietly ousted by that of the Vestry, who in 1731 ordered the old font to be restored to the Church.[n] The Rector and Churchwardens and the major part of the parishioners agreed to take proper steps "to prevent Mr. Groves from having a faculty for the seat they sit in; it being built by Lord Litchfield when he was at the Park, and being the only pew fit to accommodate gentlemen strangers."[o] On account of the tower being in a ruinous condition it was in 1759 ordered that the bells (except the Saints' Bell) should not be rung till further order;[p] in 1784 the Vestry agreed to enlarge the Singers' Gallery;[q] and in the same year the Council contracted for a new Tower to be built for £830, of which they subscribed £100.[r] We have already seen that the Grammar School was a long room adjoining the Church; when a Vestry was required in 1802, a part of the School called the Study was appropriated for that purpose, for which sixpence a year was paid to the Council.

There are no records that the Mayor ever held the Assize of Bread,[s] or the Assize of Weights and Measures during

[m] Ib., 23rd June, 1713.   [n] Churchwardens' Accounts, 22nd May, 1731.
[o] Ib., 7th May, 1738.   [p] Ib., 8th July, 1759.   [q] Ib., 11th July, 1784.
[r] Acts of Council, 13th Dec., 1784.   This tower (see illust., p. 128) is a handsome classic structure, worthy of Sir John Vanbrugh; but its present position, by the side of a Gothic church, is most incongruous.
[s] The last recorded Assize of Bread was on 25th February, 1624.

this century, although new standard weights were purchased. It should however be noted that the issues of the *Oxford Journal* for 1802 contain advertisements of numerous Assizes of Bread made by the Magistrates of the Hundred of Wootton.

In our previous chapters we have not had much to say about the Relief of the Poor, but in the eighteenth century this is a question which forces itself upon our attention. In 1756, the Vestry instructed the Churchwardens and Overseers to treat with the officers of Kidlington to know on what terms they would take the Poor of the Borough into their workhouse, and to report to the Mayor and Aldermen.[t] Later, Mr. John Rusher of Eynsham agreed to have the poor to farm in the poor-house for the sum of £140 for the space of one year;[u] in 1794 the Vestry "agreed that the care, provision, maintenance, and clothing of the poor be let to James Johnson for three years for £150, and £10 provided that at the end of the year a certificate is produced that he hath constantly clothed the poor to the satisfaction of the inhabitants";[v] but the contract was rescinded the next year by reason of Johnson's ill-treatment of the poor,[w] and a Committee was chosen to take the management of the poor into their own hands.[x] This Committee, however, was not a success, for the Churchwardens and Overseers were at the next April Vestry instructed "to borrow £120 in aid of the poor-rates by reason of great expenses incurred last year."[y] During the wars

[t] Churchwardens' Accounts, 1735-6. [u] Ib., 22nd February, 1779.
[v] Ib., 13th March, 1794. [w] Ib., 31st August, 1795.
[x] Ib., 2nd Sept., 1795. [y] Ib., 24th April, 1796.

with France the cost of maintaining the poor was enormous ; in 1796 there were eleven rates (presumably of one shilling in the pound) ; in 1801 and again in 1802 there were fifteen rates ; and in the year ending Lady Day, 1827, there were nine rates of one shilling in the pound each.

The amount raised for the relief of the poor, which was £469 in 1816, rose to £783 in 1817, and £822 in 1818 ; this large increase was explained by the break-up of the establishment at Blenheim consequent on the death of the Duke of Marlborough in 1817.[1]

There are a few instances of Medical and Out-door Relief : the Vestry " agreed to give Mr. Sotham two guineas and a half for the cure of James Smith's leg, one guinea to be paid immediately, and the other guinea and a half as soon as we are fully satisfied of the cure" ; and on the same day it was agreed to give another man " one guinea and a half towards paying his rent."[a]   But there are no entries in these accounts of money given to a man to buy boots to go to London to look for work, as there are in the Vestry books of the neighbouring parish of Combe about this time.

The View of Frankpledge met regularly during the eighteenth century ; here the Mayors produced their certificates of having communicated according to the rites of the Church of England, and took the oaths of allegiance and supremacy, although they took their oaths of office at the Council Meeting ; here the constables, tythingmen and clerks of the market (as the ale-tasters were called after 1758) were appointed, and the jury continued to present

---

[1] Municipal Corporations Commission, i, 141.
[a] Chamberlains' Accounts, 2nd April, 1758.

offenders and nuisances.' Unfortunately their presentments were not regularly entered into any book, and only odd sheets of paper containing the records of at most half-a-dozen Views have been preserved ; but we know that the jury continued to be independent of the Council, as on one occasion they ordered the Corporation to cleanse the brook within a month or pay the penalty as set by the jury,[b] and in 1828 they fined the Corporation £50 on account of the bad repair of the Causeway. On an earlier occasion[c] they had fined the constable 2s. 6d. for not keeping the pound in repair. Although the Borough Sessions were fixed for the same day as the View of Frankpledge, yet for fifty years previous to 1829 not a case had been tried in that Court[d] ; business also fell off in the Portmouth Court, for between 1820 and 1833 only twenty-four plaints were issued, and they were all compromised before coming to trial.[e]

The freemen continued to monopolize the franchises, and valued their privileges so highly as to raise the price of the freedom for an outsider to £10 in 1733[f]; they had previously ordered that if any one claimed his freedom by marriage with a freeman's widow he should pay the same fees as a compounder.[g] We have already referred to the honorary freemen ; Lord Bolingbroke[h], the Duke of York[i], Sir Joshua Reynolds[j] and Lord Clifden were voted the freedom of the Borough at various times. The Duke of

---

[b] This is found in a long entry of the View recorded in the Book of Acts of the Council in October, 1772.

[c] 10th October, 1746.

[d] Municipal Corporations Commission, 1835, i, 141.   [e] Ib.

[f] Acts of Council, 20th August, 1733.   [g] Ib., 23rd Nov., 1705.

[h] Ib., 10th Jan., 1758.   [i] Ib., 1st July, 1763.   [j] Ib., 4th Nov., 1779.

York had his freedom sent to him in a silver box, and a box of polished steel (for which Woodstock was so well known) was presented to Lord Clifden, at a cost of £37 16s. 2d.[k] Towards the end of the eighteenth century it became the custom to allow the outgoing Mayor to nominate an honorary freeman. In 1833 there were fifty-two freemen living within the Borough, twenty-four more who lived within seven miles of the Borough, and about a hundred non-resident freemen. The population in 1821 was 1455, but sank to 1380 ten years later.[l]

Towards the end of the reign of William IV the Corporation almost ceased to exist, owing in the first degree to the death of the Recorder in 1831. It appears that the Duke of Marlborough, as High Steward, claimed to nominate his successor,[m] and was supported by a number of the Council; but an almost equal number refused the Duke's claim and wished to appoint their own nominee. The Book of Acts of the Council records that on 28th September, 1831, Mr. Francis Pearson Walesby was elected Recorder in the place of Mr. James Blackstone deceased; but the Town Clerk protested against the legality of the proceedings at this meeting because it did not consist of the majority of the Council as required by the Charter. Presumably some notice was taken of this protest, and in order that this resolution might be neither confirmed nor disallowed each faction stopped away so that the

[k] Chamberlains' Accounts, 9th January, 1802.
[l] Municipal Corporations Commission, i, 141.
[m] In connection with this claim it should be noticed that it was the Duke of Marlborough (the High Steward of the Borough) who proposed the election of Mr. E. K. Lenthall, the last Recorder, on 23rd Aug., 1858.

other might not be able to elect a Recorder against their wishes ; at all events, in 1833 the Commissioners reported that the office of Recorder was vacant. Consequently the whole business of the town was neglected; as there was no Recorder no View of Frankpledge could be held ; no Chamberlains were elected during the years 1834-7 ; in the years 1834 and 1835 the new Mayor was elected at a Meeting of the Council attended by only the outgoing Mayor and the Town Clerk ; in 1836 there was no recorded election of Mayor, but Mr. Alderman Carter assumed that office in the place of Dr. Mavor, and in 1837 it is recorded that Alderman Carter "was continued as Mayor for the ensuing year, no other person having been put in nomination." The only business transacted at a Council Meeting during these four years was the distribution of Carey's clothing, and at these meetings there were never more than two present besides the Mayor and Town Clerk.

But all things, even chaos, have an end. One of the inhabitants procured a writ of mandamus to compel the Council to hold a meeting ; and in obedience to this writ a meeting was held on 19th February, 1838, at which the Mayor, Town Clerk, two Aldermen, and ten Councillors were present ; they properly elected Mr. Alderman Prior to be Mayor, and completed the number of the Council by electing two more Aldermen and seven more Councillors, and appointing two Chamberlains." And at the following meeting Mr. Walesby was sworn in as Recorder.

" For these proceedings consult Mun. Corp. Comm. i, 141, and the Acts of the Council for these years.

THE TOWN HALL AND MARKET STREET.

CHAPTER IX.

The Reign of Queen Victoria.

IT is by no means an easy task to write the history of
Woodstock during the present reign; many now
living within the town have taken no inconsiderable
part in its affairs, and one hesitates to speak of their work
for fear of occasioning offence.

The Corporation had taken a new lease of life after the
mandamus of 1838, and seems to have begun at once to set
its house in order. At a meeting held a month after the
number of the Council was completed, the members
resolved that the minutes of every meeting should be
signed by the Mayor at the next meeting, that there should

be four quarterly meetings, and that the Councillors should provide themselves with gowns;[a] notice of every motion was four days before the Council Meeting to be entered in a book provided for that purpose;[b] the salary for winding up the Town Hall clock was to be discontinued, and the Sergeant and Cryer were in the future to return their hats and cloaks if so required.[c]

The Council had not for many years exercised the power of removing its unpopular and unfit members, which it had possessed at the end of the sixteenth century.[d]   Now, however, a resolution was passed that its members were of opinion that a certain Alderman was " from his situation unfit to sit as a Magistrate of the Borough," and therefore requested " that he would see the propriety of resigning his situation as Alderman'"—a request he did not comply with for three years.[f]   The Mayor's salary of £40 a year was discontinued in 1854, and two years previously the last payment was made for refreshments to the Jury at the View of Frankpledge.[g] A resolution that the meadows should in future be let by auction to the highest bidder[h] was rescinded the following week, when it was decided that they should be allotted among the members of the Corporation as heretofore ; in 1863, however, they were thrown open to public competition,[i] and the rents at once rose to over £78.   In 1853 the Council paid £40 towards the erection of lamps in the streets, and £30 for gas for their maintenance ;[j] and there-

---

[a] Acts of Council, 19th March, 1838.   [b] Ib., 11th April, 1838.
[c] Ib., 6th Aug., 1838.   [d] See page 47.
[e] Acts of Council, 21st Dec., 1840.   [f] Ib., 23rd Sept., 1843.
[g] Chamberlains' Accounts.   [h] Acts of Council, 6th Aug., 1861.
[i] Ib., 24th Sept., 1863.   [j] Ib., 2nd June, 1853.

after till 1886 paid the bill for street lighting out of the rents of the Borough property. In 1850 the Council subscribed £100 towards the expenses of repaving the town.[k] Three years later they gave £50 towards the building fund of the National Schools;[l] and when the beneficial lease of the Cockpit was sold, in pursuance of a promise to give the land as a site for the new Schools, they paid the net proceeds, £36 10s. 9d., to the same fund.[m] They occasionally voted small subscriptions towards the expenses of the Church and of the National Schools; they gave £50 towards the stipend of the officiating Minister in 1871,[n] and £100 to the Church Restoration Fund in 1877.[o] Other charitable subscriptions were gifts of £20 for the relief of the distressed cotton operatives in Lancashire at the beginning of the winter of 1862,[p] and of £10 to the Duchess of Marlborough's Fund for the relief of the distress in Ireland in 1880.[q]

In the reign of Queen Victoria, as in the reigns of her predecessors, the Council has taken great interest in the welfare of the royal family and in contemporary politics. Addresses were voted to the Queen on the birth of the Prince of Wales, on his marriage, on the birth of his eldest son, and on his recovery from his illness in 1872; on Her Majesty's escapes from assassination in 1842 and 1882, and on other occasions. The Council "ordered that in the event of a Prince of Wales being born, the ringers be paid £1 and a hogshead of beer be given away to the poor of

---

[k] Acts of Council, 6th Feb., 1850.   [l] Ib., June, 1853.
[m] Ib., 16th April, 1855. [n] Ib., 4th Jan., 1871. [o] Ib., 3rd Aug., 1877.
[p] Ib., 4th Nov., 1862.   [q] Ib., 5th Feb., 1880.

Woodstock .... and in case of a Princess £1 be paid to the ringers."[¹] On the appointment by the Pope of a Cardinal Archbishop of Westminster in 1850, they held a special meeting, at which they adopted a series of resolutions on the subject of Papal Aggression, and presented a petition to the Queen, embodying these sentiments, and "praying her to adopt measures for the effectual repression of the assumed authority of the Pope within Her Majesty's Dominions, and for strengthening and protecting the civil and religious liberties of all Her Majesty's subjects."[ˢ] And in 1878 they passed a vote of confidence in the Government, which was entrusted to the late Lord Randolph Churchill for presentation to the Prime Minister.[ᵗ]

The affairs of the Church came into great prominence during this period. Till 1858 the Corporation of New Woodstock paid to the Churchwardens of Bladon a sum of 3s. 4d. a year as composition money—a term the meaning of which is now lost ; a similar payment of threepence a year appears in all the accounts for the early part of the seventeenth century. From a document in the handwriting of Dr. Mavor, who was then rector, it appears that the average income of the Rector of Bladon arising from the Chapelry of Woodstock for the years 1811 and 1812 amounted only to £25 4s., which sum included common fees[ᵘ] collected from every family in the town at sixpence each family, and surplice fees amounting in 1811 to £8 7s. 11d.; he also received the tithes from the Meadows and certain subscriptions amounting to about £6 10s. a

---

[¹] Ib., 2nd Nov., 1841. [ˢ] Ib., 20th Nov., 1850. [ᵗ] Ib., 7th Feb., 1878.
[ᵘ] Dr. Yule suggests that this is another term for Easter offerings.

year ; and from ancient charities the Corporation paid him
£4 12s. a year for eight sermons on fixed occasions ; but
on the other hand he derived about £400 or £500 from
the tithe and glebe in other parts of the parish.

We have seen that there is reason for supposing that in
the early part of the seventeenth century sermons were
preached at St. Mary's Church once in three weeks only ;
but at the beginning of this century service was regularly
held every Sunday morning and afternoon or evening, until
a new rector was appointed in 1847. At that time it was
thought that a clergyman with two churches in his parish
was legally bound to perform service only in one of them,
and that he had the power of closing the other at his will.
Indeed this belief was not shown to be erroneous till 1868,
when in the case of the Bishop of Winchester against Rugg
it was decided " that it is not competent to a Clerk in Holy
Orders having two churches in one benefice to perform
divine service in one only at his discretion. It is his duty
to perform a service every Sunday in each."[*] Accordingly
when a new rector was appointed in 1851, acting as he considered within his strict legal rights, he elected to perform
regular services at the Parish Church at Bladon only, and
closed the Church at Woodstock. To enable it to be re-
opened, the Duke of Marlborough, with the rector's consent,
nominated and paid a curate to perform the duties at
St. Mary's Church. This arrangement continued for twelve
years until the last curate obtained preferment in April 1862,
and then things came to a crisis. The Church was closed
for a time, and service was held in the Town Hall. The

[*] L.R. 2 Adm. and Ecc., 247.

Council wanted to eject the rector from the Rectory House on the ground that the Sunday services were not performed, but were advised that this was impossible, as the trust deed insisted only on the due performance of occasional duties ; however, the Rev. Francis Robinson, Rector of Stonesfield, for several Sundays voluntarily conducted divine service at St. Mary's Church, for which he was thanked by the Corporation." A town's meeting memorialized the Bishop, and the Duke of Marlborough again came forward and allowed his chaplains to officiate at Woodstock, for which they were remunerated by the proceeds of a voluntary subscription,[x] until a new Rector was appointed in 1876. At the present time services are held at the Church every morning and evening the whole year through.

About the year 1877 the Church was thoroughly restored at a cost of about £7,000 ; the old room which for centuries had been used as the Grammar School, was thrown into the Church and became the North Chapel, though this could not not be done without the consent of the Charity Commissioners[y] : the Corporation gallery over

[w] Acts of Council, 7th August, 1862.

[x] A similar difficulty seems to have arisen at the end of the seventeenth century, as appears from the following memorandum in the earliest Register of Births, &c. :—

" Memorandum.—That upon a controversy between the Rector of Bladon and the town of Woodstock, the Rector of Bladon not thinking himself subject to maintain a resident preaching chaplain for the town, or to allow more than the profits accruing and growing due within the chapelry, and the town refusing to subscribe more, and declining the prosecution of the matter in the Bishop's Court, the Right Hon. James, late Earl of Abingdon, and after his decease in 1698 the Right Hon. Montagu, Earl of Abingdon, were pleased severally to allow and pay to Henry Meux, Clerk, the sum of £20 per annum for serving the Chapel from the 1st day of August, 1695, to Michaelmas, 1702."

[y] Acts of Council, 3rd August, 1877.

the chancel arch looking down into the nave was removed, as were the other galleries over the arches between the nave and the aisles : the chancel was properly fitted up, and the pulpit removed from the middle to the east end of the nave, while new seats were substituted for the hideous old box pews. The Corporation contributed £100 to this work, but it would never have been completed but for the untiring energies of the late rector, the Rev. Arthur Majendie.

An inquiry held by the Municipal Corporations Commission in 1877[1] shows that in the course of years the mode of election of the Mayor had again been changed. By the orders of 1580 he was to be elected by the freemen from the Aldermen on the nomination of the Council[a]; by the Charter of 1665 he was to be elected from the Aldermen by the Mayor and Commonalty or the major part of them[b]; but in 1877, as the evidence shows, he was elected from the Aldermen by the freemen on the nomination of a freeman.[c] In practice the Council decided who should be the new Mayor and gave the hint to the freemen; but on one occasion within the last thirty years the freemen disregarded this hint and elected another man as Mayor. Every freeman who was not a member of the Council received a refreshment ticket of the value of three shillings and sixpence for attending the election of Mayor. The number of freemen had gradually decreased, until in 1885 only four attended the election. The last recorded admission

---

[1] Municipal Corporations Commission, vol. ii, pp. 247, 851.
[a] See page 33.   [b] See page 94.
[c] This appears to have been the practice in 1833 (Report of Municipal Corporations Commission, i, 141); and the surviving members of the old Corporation corroborate the Report.

of hereditary freemen at a Council meeting was on the 19th September, 1864, when two were admitted as being the eldest sons of their fathers. It will be remembered that none but freemen could be members of the Council; and every outsider who was wanted on the Council was made an honorary freeman before he could be elected a Common Councillor; the last of these honorary freemen was made in 1882. But the honorary freemen had no right to share in the charities for the benefit of the freemen; these consisted of several sums of money, amounting to about £400, which till 1844 had been lent to the freemen in small sums without interest for a certain number of years; but in that year the sum of three pounds, being the interest and compound interest on the dole they would have received, was given to every freeman who applied, and the balance was invested[d]; and this practice was followed every five years.

The Corporation in 1842 declined to recognise any liability in respect of the Fire Engine,[e] and shifted that liability to the Vestry, who continued to manage it till the Volunteer Fire Brigade was formed in 1871.

The last business transacted at the Portmouth Court was on the 1st February, 1847, when William Pain was admitted a freeman as the eldest son of his father. The Court met for the last time on 5th July in that year, after which it was superseded by the new County Court. The last recorded meeting of the View of Frankpledge was on 1st April, 1853; no salary was paid to the Recorder after Michaelmas, 1864; and the last Council Meeting of the

[d] Acts of Council, 12th Nov., 1844.   [e] Ib., 5th May, 1842.

Mayor and Commonalty of the Borough of New Woodstock was held on 6th May, 1886. At Michaelmas in the next year the old Corporation expired, and the property passed on 9th November, 1886, to a new body elected by the householders of an extended area under the laws governing. Municipal Corporations generally. The Mayor and Aldermen continued to act as the Licensing Justices for the Borough till the new Corporation came into power, but the County Justices are now the Licensing authority.

It would ill become one who is the servant of the new Corporation to criticise its acts and deeds. True its members have discarded the gowns and robes of their predecessors, and have thus lost much of the picturesque effect which was always produced by a state procession of the older body; but every one will acknowledge that in zeal for the improvement of the town and the good of its inhabitants the new Corporation is far superior to the old, even in its palmiest days before the Civil War.

OLD WOODSTOCK.

APPENDIX A.

—

Old Woodstock.

THE hamlet of Old Woodstock, lying along the main Oxford and Birmingham road by the side of the Park wall to the north of the Borough of New Woodstock, was never included within the boundaries of the old Borough. Old Woodstock was part of the ecclesiastical parish of Wootton ; while New Woodstock was part of the parish of Bladon. Old Woodstock has always been parcel of the Manor of Woodstock ; and to-day its quit-rents are collected by the Duke of Marlborough, while the quit-rents of New Woodstock are collected by the Corporation.

As Old Woodstock is parcel of the Manor of Woodstock, its copyholds, of which there are a fair number, are subject to the peculiar customs regulating inheritance which apply to the whole manor ; from an old custumal of the manor in the British Museum[a] we learn that the lands within the manor were divided into free, customary, Bury and Sart lands ; and that on the death of any copyhold tenant the free lands descended to the eldest son, while the customary, Bury, and Sart lands went to the youngest son, according to the well-known custom of Borough English : and to this day certain of the properties descend to the eldest and others to the youngest son.   Every one knows that the custom of Borough English is a Saxon custom ; may we not therefore argue that in the recesses of the Forest of Woodstock the Saxon families survived the Norman conquest in such strength as to be able to retain their old customs in the face of their conquerors ?

Another custom observed in Old Woodstock, even within the last few years, was the election of the Mayor of Old Woodstock, on the Feast Day, the Monday following the first Sunday after September 19th.   In the morning there used to be a cricket match and sports, followed at mid-day by a dinner at the " Rose and Crown " public-house ; after dinner the Mayor was elected, and in the evening he was chaired down Old Woodstock and round New Woodstock, stopping at all the public-houses on the way.   Frequently his retinue finished the proceedings by dropping him into the river Glyme at the bottom of Old Woodstock hill.   A number of instances of this custom have been met with in Cornwall ; and a similar custom is to be found in many parts of India.   In the latter case the mock Chieftain is always elected by the subject races.[b]

[a] Lansdowne MSS. No. 758.

[b] G. L. Gomme : Village Community, 105-115, where the whole subject is fully discussed.

We have already referred to the tradition that Old Woodstock was founded in the reign of Henry I, when he formed the park and surrounded it with a stone wall. The hamlet is one of those places that has no history ; except that the Black Prince is said to have resided in the old Manor House, which now belongs to Balliol College.[c] But the name of this property in the fourteenth century was Praunce's Place.[d]

When the area of the borough was extended in 1886, the hamlet of Old Woodstock was included within its boundaries, and it is now a separate civil parish by virtue of the Local Government Act, 1894. It had previously been separated ecclesiastically from the parish of Wootton, and joined to Bladon-cum-Woodstock in 1877.

Old Woodstock is famous as being the birthplace of the celebrated strain of " Blenheim Orange " apples. Tradition says that the Birmingham coaches used to stop for a minute to allow the passengers to gaze on the first " Blenheim Orange " tree.

[c] Marshall, p. 97.　　[d] Archives of Balliol College.

APPENDIX B.

The Assize of Bread and Beer.

Burgus NOVE WOODSTOCK } THE **Courte** of Wm Meatcalfe, gent., Maior of the said Borowe, and allso Clarke of the Markett there houlden at the Guild hall on Wensday the sixth of September in the seconde yeere of the reigne of o^r Sovereigne lo : kinge Charles &c. 1626.

Jur pro dnō Rege

Bennett Painter
Tho Woodward
Edw Hull
Robt Spittle
John Sea
Henry Whitfield

}

Thomas Heddy
Edw Johnson
Johes Don
Edw Silver
Johes Durbridge
Tho. Godfrey

} **Jur.**

It. the Jurors doe present the best wheate to be worth by the quarter ... ... 40s.

It. the second wheate by the quarter ... 32s.

It. the best mault by the quarter ... ... 29s. 4d.

It. the second mault by the quarter ... 26s. 8d.

The Maior afores^d chardgeth and comaundeth all bakers, brewers, and victulers to keepe the assize follow-inge vizt :

It. the penny white loffe to way ... 8 oz. & dimid.

It. the penny wheaten loffe to way ... 13 oz.

It. the penny howshold to way ... 17 oz.

It. the Barrell of the strongest Beere not to be sould for above ... 9s. 8d.

It. a kilderkin for beere not to be sould for above ... ... 4s. 10d.

It. everie Inholder and Victuler to sell an Ale quarte of beere and ale for 1d.

And twoe quarts of small drinke for a 1d.

The Jurors afores^d doe finde and present that Xtofer Smith diverse tymes did want 2 & 3 oz. in his bread of the last assize. Ideo* ... ... 13s. 4d.

It. that James Nickolls did wante 2 oz. in his wheaten bread and hath broake the Assize in all of his bread baiking. Ideo ... ... 13s. 4d.

It. John Bignell did the like many tymes. Ideo ... ... 6s. 8d.

(Signed)
WILLIAM MEATCALFE, *Maior.*
EDMOND HIORNE [*Town Clerk.*]

* Supply " est in Amerciamenta."

APPENDIX C.

Woodstock Gloves.

THE order of the View of Frankpledge of 1580[a] incidentally referred to the gloving industry, and from that time till now Woodstock gloves have had a more than local fame. Queen Elizabeth, on one of her visits, graciously accepted gloves from the Woodstock glovers; and it is said that that pair of her gloves which is preserved in the Ashmolean Museum at Oxford is of Woodstock manufacture.

In 1616 the University of Oxford presented James I with a pair of very rich gloves made at Woodstock, and at the present time there are some half-a-dozen glove manufacturers in the town.

The gloves are of two kinds; the one, the old-fashioned Woodstock glove, is made of English sheep and lamb skins, which are specially prepared by fellmongers at a distance; after the skins are brought into the town they are pared, grounded, and bleached, often by being exposed on the hedges at the sides of one of the roads leading into the

[a] See page 71.

town, and afterwards coloured. The tan driving-gloves are made of sheep-skins from Australia and the Cape of Good Hope, tanned and prepared by a peculiar method, in which the yolk of eggs procured from Russia, Normandy, and Ireland plays an important part.

Part of the operation of cutting out gloves is done by hand and part by press. In some factories the gloves are machine-sewn by women workers, but more frequently they are sent out into the neighbouring villages to be sewn by hand by the women and girls, who thus add a few shillings weekly to the earnings of their husbands and fathers who are mostly agricultural labourers. Some women even earn more than their husbands.

It is estimated that about two thousand women and girls thus work at gloving in the district, and it is remarkable that by far the greater part of this work is done in those villages that are within or on the borders of the Forests of Cornbury, Woodstock, and Wychwood : outside these villages there are very few gloveresses. The reason for the connection between the gloving industry and the forests is to be found in the fact that the earliest gloves were made of the skins of the deer which had been killed in the forests.

One or two firms make a speciality of cricket and athletic goods, but it is generally admitted that the staple trade of the town has been to some extent injured by the high protective duties imposed by the United States.

INDEX.

—

PRINTED BY
ALDEN AND COMPANY, LTD.,
35 CORN-MARKET STREET,
OXFORD.

BY THE SAME AUTHOR.

NOTES on the HISTORY of CHIPPING-NORTON,
By Adolphus Ballard, B.A., LL.B. Demy 8vo. Price One
Shilling.
  Oxford : Alden & Co. Ltd., Bocardo Press.

"Mr. Adolphus Ballard, B.A., LL.B. (London), has recently
published a monograph on the historical records of Chipping Norton,
which reflects the greatest credit on his industry and scholarship in
working in the fruitful field of local history and antiquities. Such
labour expended in studying original records leads us to expect that
Mr. Ballard will in the future do still more valuable work in
archæology and history."—*Methodist Times.*

From F. W. Maitland, Esq., LL.D., *Downing Professor of Law
  in the University of Cambridge.*

    "Downing College, Cambridge,
       "*10th Dec., 1893.*
"Dear Sir,
 "Please accept my best thanks for the copy of your interesting
'Notes on Chipping Norton' that you were kind enough to send me.
I hope that you will continue your researches. The history of our
smaller boroughs is still very obscure.
    "Believe me,
      "Yours very sincerely,
       "F. W. MAITLAND."

RANDOLPH HOTEL,
OXFORD.
In the Centre of the City.

Opposite the Martyrs' Memorial.

THE only modern-built Hotel in Oxford, close to the Colleges and Public Buildings. A few minutes' walk from the Railway Stations, River, Theatre, &c.

Handsome Suites of Rooms. **Ladies' Coffee Room.**
Ball Room. **Billiard Rooms.** **Smoking Rooms.**
General Drawing Room, and every convenience.

LIGHTED BY ELECTRICITY.

A Night Porter in attendance. *Charges Moderate.*

ADDRESS: THE MANAGER

THE MITRE HOTEL,
OXFORD.

KNOWN and frequented for centuries by many generations of Oxonians and Tourists, is situated in the
best part of the High Street, and is

One of the most Economical First=Class Hotels in the Kingdom.

This old-established and comfortable House has recently
undergone enlargements which have greatly increased its
Coffee Room and Dining Room accommodation. It is
fitted throughout with Electric Light, and by the addition
of a number of Bed Rooms and Bath Rooms it is now in
a position to meet the requirements of Visitors.

Early application should be made to
THE MANAGER.

BLENHEIM PARK RESTAURANT,

WOODSTOCK.

(CLOSE TO THE PARK GATES.)

Dinners, Teas, &c., provided.
PARTIES ACCOMMODATED.

S. LEGGATT, PROPRIETRESS.

FOR

GENUINE

Woodstock Gloves,

Direct from the Makers,

GO TO

HENRY COLLETT,

Draper, &c.,

MARKET STREET,

WOODSTOCK.

Printed in the United Kingdom by
Lightning Source UK Ltd., Milton Keynes
138740UK00001B/39/P